THE SOUND OF BURNING

CRUX
THE GEORGIA SERIES IN LITERARY NONFICTION

The Sound of Burning

A MOTHER, A DAUGHTER, A MURDER

Kristi D. Osorio

THE UNIVERSITY OF GEORGIA PRESS · ATHENS

Athens, Georgia 30602
www.ugapress.org

Designed by Erin Kirk
Set in Arno
Printed and bound by Sheridan Books

The paper in this book meets the guidelines for permanence and durability of the Committee on Production Guidelines for Book Longevity of the Council on Library Resources.

Printed in the United States of America
26 27 28 29 30 P 5 4 3 2 1

EU Authorized Representative
Easy Access System Europe—Mustamäe tee 50, 10621
Tallinn, Estonia, gpsr.requests@easproject.com

Library of Congress Control Number: 2026018178
ISBN 9780820378091 (paperback)
ISBN 9780820378107 (epub)
ISBN 9780820378114 (PDF)

For my brother,
who held my hand

I have a story to tell. It is a story of murders: murders of the flesh, and of the spirit; murders born of heartbreak, of hatred, of retribution. It is the story of where those murders begin, of how they take form and enter our actions, how they transform our lives, how their legacies spill into the world and the history around us. And it is a story of how the claims of violence and murder end—if indeed, they ever end. I know this story well, because I have been stuck inside it.

—Mikal Gilmore, *Shot in the Heart*

I was sixteen for twenty years.

—Lucie Brock-Broido, "A Girl Ago"

CONTENTS

AUTHOR'S NOTE

This work relies heavily on my own memory, which is a fraught thing in the aftermath of a traumatic event that occurred during adolescence. The scenes and dialogue throughout are reconstructed from my memory and archival artifacts, including court transcripts, police records, letters, and newspaper articles. Several instances of dialogue have been pulled directly from such records, while others are based on memory alone. Where possible, I have also relied on the memories of others who were involved to re-create moments from the past. I have attempted to render each person here wholly and truthfully based on facts and memories; it was not my intention to speak on their behalf or make assumptions about their beliefs or experiences. A violent event like the one in this book has far-reaching effects that don't end for the family, friends, or community when the investigation does. As such, some names and identifying characteristics have been changed out of respect for the privacy of those involved. Names appearing in legal records and newspaper articles have been altered.

PROLOGUE

At first, I didn't know she was dead. Killed. At first, I thought, well, maybe the house is on fire. The screams sounded impossible, the *help me, help me, somebody please.* She kept saying, *I'm burning.* Over and over, not just once. We'd lost another house in a fire in the first grade, Barbie dolls seared, plastic bodies smelling like a tire smoking on the side of some major highway. I knew then, when I buried what was left of Skipper and Ken, that none of us could outlive a flame.

But there was no fire. No smoke, not a single flame. It was something else entirely: a killing. A slaying, as they'd call it in the newspapers hours later. There had been some knife or blade, some unknown sharp thing, lost, thrown out, abandoned. Some say Mom hid it when she ran out the front door, her T-shirt stained like someone who'd just done something bad.

Am I in trouble? I wanted to ask as if it were my shirt. *Am I in trouble?* I still ask sometimes when I think of that night. The gray knees of Mom's sweatpants were red with her own mother's blood, too, but I hadn't seen them yet. When I watched her run across the gravel driveway, shoeless, hysterical, I went to Nick's room.

Was she running from something or chasing it?

Something's wrong with Betty, I said, or maybe I shouted.

I was fifteen, my brother eighteen. There were so many things we didn't know. How to tell when a murder is happening down the hall. How to stop it from happening. How to call 9-1-1 and tell them your address.

I had picked up the house phone, somehow dialed the numbers. But I couldn't believe when there was a live human person on the other end, that this wasn't just some movie where something is going terribly wrong. When I finally spoke, I gave the dispatcher the wrong address, sounding like a little girl who was lost and looking for a grown-up to take over and do the scary stuff.

There were so many things I didn't know then and so many that I'll never understand.

How my room was on the way to *the scene,* the place where my grandmother once slept, matching Betty Boop lamps on either side of her bed. How she was the one to die, but the three of us lived. How, after I got Nick, he kept me from seeing, told me not to walk back into the room where it happened. How Mom stood there after, screaming, dazed, unhinged, unbelievable, like a cartoon drawing of a crazy person.

We're all going to die, she kept saying to no one. She must have taken one of her pills, one of her tranquilizers, as she always called them.

There's fucking blood everywhere, Nick said to the dispatcher, afraid to check a pulse, afraid to touch the dead body because he loved her. Because she wasn't just a body. He didn't want her to leave.

What's this? Mom asked me, looking down at the blood on her shirt. *What's all over me?* she asked, rocking back and forth. *Who are you?* she asked, her eyes so glossy they turned black.

PART ONE A Killing

Cigarette smoke clung to everything. Our furniture and our clothes and even our walls reeked of it, but I never noticed until I left home. Some mornings after Nick drove me to school, I'd sit in first period suddenly overwhelmed by my own scent. Mom and Betty, who only ever let us call her Betty, always had cigarettes in their hands. It was almost like they took turns: Mom lit a new one up as soon as Betty put an old one out, rinse and repeat until the day was done. They made Nick disconnect all the smoke detectors when we moved into the house, Betty explained, so she and Mom could smoke as much as they wanted without the goddamn alarm going off.

On the nights when Mom, Betty, and I were home together, they would take drags from their cigarettes while we watched recorded episodes of *Jeopardy!* and *Law & Order: Special Victims Unit*, passing around a bowl of popcorn or taking turns stirring the pot of powdered Jell-O pudding on the stove. As we fast-forwarded through the commercials on the DVR, sometimes I'd look up to see where the smoke alarm used to be, its colored wires still dangling from the ceiling above us. It wouldn't have been stupid to think a fire had come that night. But it hadn't.

We'd been watching *Law & Order* for years, and even though every episode followed the same plot structure—after the voice told us about the *heinous crimes* and the famous *dun-dun* followed—we were obsessed. We watched episode after episode, talking loudly through each one, turning minor characters into suspects and deciding who'd done the unthinkable act we'd watched in the opening scene. It was almost like what happened in the show didn't matter—we cared more about our own theories and about which one of us would be right when the truth was finally revealed. There were some episodes whose resolutions we didn't buy, and some that caused screaming matches about who was right. The two of them would resort to Google searches about how to kill someone using a certain kind of method or weapon. There was something special about the three of us watching it, alone, without any men—not even Nick. We'd joke about how we'd be experts if we ever had a case of our own to crack, how we felt sorry for any man who'd ever try to attack any of us.

We'd outsmart the fucker in an instant, Betty would say, laughing with an inch-long ash hanging off the edge of her cigarette.

We lived in a small, rural desert town. The only thing people went there for was the casino where Betty worked. The nearest movie theater was almost twenty minutes away and the mall was at least thirty. I had my learner's permit, but I was still too young to drive without an adult, so I mostly relied on my brother to take me places. Nick had worked at the supermarket near the casino for a few years, and he and his friends spent weekends all the way out in Albuquerque, making the hour-and-a-half-long trip alongside speeding semitrucks, going to hardcore shows, flirting with girls they met on Myspace. Some nights I'd spend hours on the computer, looking at pictures of the girls online, their hair long and their lips pierced and their eyes covered in perfect black eyeliner.

It was Nick's senior year, and most of the time, he would stay out all night, coming home only after dropping all his friends off and stumbling into bed just to sleep for a couple of hours before he had to clock in at work. He still got good grades, tutored middle school kids in his spare time. Around town, people always called me Nick's Little Sister or Betty's Granddaughter or A.D.'s Daughter. They all knew Nick because he bagged their groceries. They knew Betty because she was the casino's only foul-mouthed, poker-dealing grandmother. They knew Mom because she'd worked at almost every place in town—the casino, the gas station, the Dairy Queen, the video store, and even the high school—at some point since we'd moved there. And they remembered her because she was beautiful.

Some afternoons I'd go to the casino after school to meet Betty so we could ride home together. She was almost always at the casino, even when she wasn't working, until it was time to head home to watch the DVR. I liked walking through the tunnels of slot machines, their lights blazing blue and red and gold all around me, announcing losses and victories with the sound of coins clinking and crashing. With my backpack slung over one shoulder, I felt grown up in those clouds of cigarette smoke and rows of people with lifeless eyes glued to the blinking screens promising them a big win.

When I thought of the casino, I thought of Betty. It was hers. There was only one thing about that place that I hated: the men. Usually, as I'd pass by the blackjack tables and the wheeled carts filled with bottles and cans of alcohol, some strange man I'd never met would ask me about Mom.

Hey, how's she doin'? they'd ask. *I'm a friend of hers, you know. I bet she told you about me.* I'd smile politely enough and talk to them, smelling the drinks on their breath, trying to make it look like I was in a rush to get going somewhere, anywhere. I was used to doing things like that, talking to guys when they wanted to talk to Mom. I'd spent years answering the phone for her just to tell another guy that she wasn't here right now or that he had the wrong number.

There's no one by that name here, I'd say, trying not to laugh, following the instructions she gave when she coached me. Sometimes, when the guy was a total loser, she'd even let me tell them she was dead.

Rio Grande Sun
May 15, 2008

Chilling Account of Nambé Woman's Murder

In her booking photo, A.D. looks young for her 44 years but she is certainly not childlike. She has feathered brown hair that lands just off her shoulders, ribbony eyebrows, a long, slender neck, and a face the shape of a perfect oval. Seen outside of a mugshot, many might easily describe her as pretty. But in the police photo her gaze still shows the effect of the clonazepam, an anti-seizure and anti-anxiety medication she had taken before police arrived, court documents state.

When I'd thought there was a fire, I pictured men in big yellow jackets coming to rescue me like they did on screen. Maybe they'd pull me out of my bed and unravel the hose from their red truck in the gravel driveway. Maybe we'd be on the front page of the paper.

Family of four survives housefire. Cause remains unknown.

Or maybe: *Local casino creep(s) suspected of arson.*

Mom had sat me down for a talk about a week earlier. On the edge of my bed, where we would later wait for the police to arrive, she told me our neighborhood was getting more and more *dangerous*. Our house was on a narrow dirt trail off a winding, paved road that was mostly empty, except for a few adobe houses and the occasional double-wide trailer. When we first moved in, some kids at my high school said, *You know you live across the street from a meth lab, right?*

Make sure you lock your window every night, Mom said, although I couldn't remember ever opening it in the first place. *This group of guys has been going around breaking into cars. I just want you to be safe.*

Down the street from our house lived Mom's on-again, off-again boyfriend. He had tan skin, green eyes, and a little black box strapped around his ankle. Everyone knew his family was in the meth business. Everyone knew, too, that, when Mom started dating him, he had recently been released from a ten-year prison sentence.

He's clean now, she said when Betty and I questioned her about going out with him. Nick grew frustrated with their relationship, embarrassed. Everyone knew everyone in our town. And everyone knew the kind of guy our mother was sleeping with.

When the screaming started, the *I'm burning,* the blue glow of my cell phone said it was Tuesday, 1:58 a.m. I still had four more hours until my alarm clock was supposed to wake me up to get ready for school. Everyone was asleep inside their homes, too far away to have heard the screams coming from inside ours. With the smoke alarms disconnected, no one would notice until morning if the flames swallowed us whole.

I was the youngest in the house, the baby. Mom and Betty were adults, Nick was practically one himself. I didn't want to be the one to get up first, discover whatever the bad thing was. I kept waiting to hear one of their doors open, wishing one of them would come and tell me everything was fine. I still don't know how, but finally, I dug myself out from under my blanket and opened the bedroom door. The hall outside my room was dark except for the faint blue light coming from Mom's TV on the other side of her half-open door. She wasn't in her bed. She wasn't anywhere.

From the other side of the house, I could hear the crying now, the *No, no, no. We're all going to die.* It was dark when I walked into Betty's room, but I could still see Mom, shaking, standing over something on the right side of the bed. Even though I couldn't see color, I already knew her pale cheeks were flushed red like they always were when she panicked. But I had never seen her like this before. Her voice sounded like it belonged to someone else, someone I'd never met.

Or maybe I had.

If I had thought to turn on the light, I would have seen the bloodstained sheets on Betty's bed, a hardcover mystery novel with a dog-eared page near her pillow. I would have seen her on the floor, lying between Mom's legs in a pool of blood on the tile the two of them had picked out to match the blinds hanging from the windows in every room. But Mom was crying harder and louder now, making sounds I never knew anyone could make, saying again that we were all going to die. So the light stayed off, even when Mom ran outside.

Nick stood beside me in his white T-shirt and watched when Mom walked back up to the house with only darkness behind her. There were no streetlights in our neighborhood, only square adobe houses with flat roofs and wooden beams that matched the coyote fences separating their yards from ours. With the front door open, there was finally some light coming in from the single bulb on the front porch we'd left on before bed. The night was black behind Mom as she leaned against the doorframe in one of the oversized shirts she wore when she colored her hair with boxed dye from Walmart.

Mom, what the fuck is all over you? Nick asked, looking up and down. My eyes widened. There was something splattered across her shirt, wet, dark, and patchy like stains from a sloppy dye job, but I would have noticed if she'd been leaning over the side of the tub with her head under the faucet in the middle of the night. That's when I saw the dark circles on the knees of her gray sweatpants, as if she'd kneeled in something wet on the ground when she ran outside. It hadn't rained that night.

> [The suspect] stated she ran out of the home and went to the neighbors to call the police. . . . I made contact with [redacted] the neighbor to [*sic*] A.D. stated she went for help. [Redacted] stated that no one came to her door on the morning the incident occurred. She stated that the only thing she saw was rescue and police arrive on scene.
>
> —Santa Fe County Sheriff's Department Offense Report, May 14, 2008

Nick told me to take Mom to my room while he went into Betty's, where I'd soon hear him shout, *Fuck, oh fuck,* into the phone while the 9-1-1 dispatcher told him to hold Betty's bleeding body in his arms and check her pulse. Mom was shaking and crying now, her knees pushed up to her chest, rocking back and forth with her fingers braided together as if to pray.

It's going to be okay, I repeated every few minutes, trying to speak slowly and calmly. *Don't worry, Mom.* It almost came out *Mommy,* a name I hadn't used in years. I had seen Mom have panic attacks before, at the grocery store or in the car on a busy highway or in the school supplies aisle at Walmart, but I'd never seen one like this before. As I stood in my pajamas trying to comfort her like I always had, she looked so small to me, crying, *No, no, no.* I left my room only once, to get Mom a glass of water from the kitchen sink to try to calm her down. She reached up to take the glass, and her shaking hands dropped it, splashing water on herself.

Watch out, Mom, I said, annoyed. My backpack was next to her along with the biology presentation I had to turn in the next day. She looked down at herself and saw the blood on her clothes for what seemed like the first time.

What's this? she asked. *What's all over my shirt? What is happening to me?* She stood up, keeping her eyes on the stains on her shirt.

Am I bleeding? she finally cried. I didn't know how to answer her.

That was when I saw the blood on her hands: light red now, dried inside the creases of her small, manicured fingers.

When Nick finally came back from Betty's room for the last time, the front of his white shirt was stained with blood. It wasn't stained the way Mom's shirt was. It was smeared, like he had wiped his hand across his chest after he and the voice on the other end of the phone realized there was nothing he could do.

I pictured Nick on the ground with Betty: maybe he had to hold the phone up to his ear with his shoulder as he followed the instructions to place two fingers on her neck and try to find a beat. I thought of how all I did when I heard the first scream was hide in my room waiting for it to fill up with smoke from some imaginary house fire, trying to wish the noise away.

Help would be there soon, Nick said, and he joined Mom and me on my bed and wrapped his arms around us, the two of them wearing Betty's blood on their shirts. I couldn't remember the last time the three of us had been so close. I almost felt sad when the moment was interrupted, the red and blue lights shining through the blinds on my bedroom window. Suddenly, an image came to my mind: the four of us—Betty, alive—sitting outside watching our house burn down as the fire truck finally pulled in.

Mom went to the sink, took off her shirt, and started rinsing the blood off her hands.

You, she said, looking down, then at me. *Y-y-you have to help me clean it.*

There was so much blood that when she peeled the shirt off, it had already stuck to her skin. I felt disgusting, monstrous, indecent, looking at the red stains on her naked torso when the police walked in.

The men with guns strapped to their waists and flashlights in their hands started walking around inside the house and outside in the yard.

I think I went on a date with him once, Mom said in a zombielike hum, pointing at one of the cops.

I know you, he said.

Betty was still alone in her room, lying on the floor where Nick had sat with her. There were no more screams. No sounds at all from inside her room. Nick had told them it was like a *howl,* a sound he'd never heard before in his life.

In the living room, a group of officers circled around me like I'd done something wrong, each of them asking the same questions I didn't want to answer anymore.

What was your relationship to the victim?

Had your mother and the victim gotten into any fights recently?

Would you mind speaking up, a little louder please?

Did the two of them ever yell, get into big arguments, anything like that?

Can you tell me again what time you heard the first scream?

Can you repeat that?

To your knowledge, are there any weapons in the house?

I knew Mom had a gun in her room—a 9-millimeter she kept in the closet, tucked away in a little box. But there'd been no gunshots; I was sure of it. There was a list of sharp objects, things they found in every drawer, every closet, every place you'd never dare to look in a house that doesn't belong to you. The cops took eight knives out of the house from the dishwasher and the kitchen drawers. They took my scissors, protractor, and compass off my desk, sealed them in a bag labeled *evidence.* I was still on track to fail geometry with or without the protractor and compass, but I never got them back.

Nick was in another room being asked the same questions by different officers, and Mom was in the living room, in a purple bathrobe now, smoking on the couch. It was as if she was waiting for something. She seemed calmer now, put her hand on the cushion to her left, motioned for me to sit beside her. I looked around at the officers, busy shining their flashlights inside the washing machine and dryer. Maybe I didn't want to sit with her. Maybe I did. As Mom put her cigarette out in an ashtray Nick had made for her in a ceramics class when he was little, I sat gently, trying not to make a sound. When I looked down at her hands, I imagined wet blood on her fingers, seeping through the white paper wrapped around the cigarette as she crushed the glowing cherry into a black pile.

After the officers made us leave the house for the investigation, Nick and I were placed in separate police cars parked along the driveway. Through our windows, we watched Mom pace back and forth through the gravel as the officers tried to calm her down again. The lights from the cars flashed against the window to Betty's room, and I could see shadows walking around inside, looking at the blood on the walls and shining their flashlights on the dark places they couldn't see. Did any neighbors look outside, peer through their windows, just to see where all the lights were coming from? Did they see us sitting there, two siblings in cop cars, a mother wailing in her bathrobe?

I sunk down on the black vinyl seat and lay down across it with my feet up against the window. Why did Betty say *help me, I'm burning*? All I wanted was to go to sleep so I could be on time for school. I was trying to get my grade up in biology class, and I was supposed to give a presentation that afternoon.

Did anyone already ask you if there were weapons in the house? asked one of the younger officers after he opened the car door. He got into the front seat and said he would be taking me to the police station in Santa Fe and that Nick and Mom would be on their way there, too.

Weapons? I thought of the men from the casino. Did one of them have something to do with this? Did one of them break into our house and hurt Betty? Did some *shithead,* some *loser,* finally get fed up waiting around for

Mom to notice him? Everything was moving so fast I couldn't keep my thoughts straight. Why would someone hurt Betty?

You'll probably get some time off from school, the officer said. *I did when my grandma died.*

When our house had burned down, back when we lived in North Carolina, Mom told us it was because of faulty wiring in the attic. Nick and I were little then, devastated to lose our Hot Wheels, our Barbies, our bunkbed, and our stuffed animals. The room where we'd imitate our favorite WWF wrestlers fighting cage matches and watch *Brady Bunch* reruns on Nick at Nite was gone forever. Later, some neighbors said Mom was acting strangely that week, that they'd seen her coming in and out of the house with bins and trash bags in the days before the fire.

As I sat in the back of the police car, it seemed impossible that Betty was not alive anymore, that she had been lying on the floor of her room, dead the whole time. I didn't want to picture what she might have looked like in there, where exactly all that blood had come from, and why. I tried to think of what she looked like the day before, when she was alive, smoking on the couch like she did every day.

You'd never smoke one of these fuckin' things, would ya, Kris? she asked sometimes.

She always wore bright shades of lipstick, and her hair was cut into a boyish brown crop with bold blonde streaks around her face. She wore almost the same outfit every single day: jeans with a long-sleeve shirt and a vest colored with quirky patterns or embroidery or beads that made strangers stop and talk to her at the post office or the casino parking lot. In the mornings, she sprayed the inside of her wrists with a black bottle of gardenia perfume and drove to work in her stick-shift Jeep, the least grandmotherly car in the world. Betty knew I would never smoke a cigarette, just as I'd never dare call her *Grandma.*

She wasn't like other people's grandmothers. She didn't wear sweaters or pick me up on time or bake cookies for my friends. Everyone always commented on how different, how eccentric she was. Kids whose parents knew her from the casino would tell me how hilarious she was, how every other word out of her mouth was *fuck* or *shit* and she didn't even seem to notice. We had lived with her since Mom's second split from our stepdad, Craig, the four of us in our little house with the turquoise door in this tiny town.

When the officer pulled out of the driveway to take me to the police station, I turned to look back at the house one last time like they do in movies. There were more cars in the driveway now, more men walking in and out of the front door. The sun would come up soon, but there was a darkness that lingered over the police cars, the crew scouring the perimeter. Past the Jeep, the yellow caution tape surrounded the yard with the big black words we'd seen so many times during our *Law & Order* marathons on the couch: CRIME SCENE. DO NOT CROSS.

How long have you lived with the victim? asked the detective who'd been assigned to the case. He had a tattoo of tiny black marks circling his wrist. I couldn't quite make them out. In the bright light of the interrogation room, no one looked good. It had been about four years, give or take. For a year in fifth grade, after the first separation. Then for three or so after the separation and again after the official divorce. *Who would take care of us now?* I wondered, a question that made me feel stupid, childish. We hadn't lived with Mom alone since we were little, right after the house burned down. There was always someone else. Our parents hadn't been together in years, but there were always boyfriends, then Craig, and then Betty.

While the detective questioned me, I stared at myself in the same one-way mirror I'd seen on all my favorite TV shows. I wondered who was on the other side, watching and listening, writing down the words I said and the way my voice sounded when I said them. It felt like one of those old black-and-white crime shows where the cop shined a bright light into the bad guy's face until he said the right thing. My skin was washed out, almost translucent, and the circles under my eyes were light blue like two small bruises. I'd only known a couple of people who had died: a girl from the Boys and Girls Club in elementary school and one of my classmates who got into a car accident the previous year. Nobody I loved, nobody in my immediate family, had ever died before. I didn't know what I was supposed to feel, how I was supposed to look, what I was supposed to say.

Somehow, I hadn't cried yet, not even back at the house when I first heard that Betty was dead. I'd been in the driveway locked in the back of the police car for so long I started to fall asleep, but then, the young-looking officer opened the door just to tell me she was gone. Even then, I was too tired to feel anything. What kind of person falls asleep at a crime scene?

Now, hours later, I was tired of being alone, locked up inside this office like I was in trouble for something when I didn't even know what I'd done. I wanted to know where Nick and Mom were, if they were locked inside their own offices, being asked the same questions I was being forced to answer again. My mind kept replaying the screams coming from Betty's room, the blood on Mom's shirt.

So, the detective continued. *Do you know what happened last night?*

All I knew for certain was that Betty had died, that there had been a lot of blood when it happened. I kept looking down at my hands and peeled the glitter polish off my nails. I was embarrassed about the way I looked, still wearing the pajamas I'd worn to bed the night before.

He asked me the same question in different words, as all the officers had been doing all night since they first pulled into the driveway. I didn't know why his tone made me feel so stupid, small, scared. I knew I hadn't done anything wrong. I didn't think that anyone could have done anything wrong. It had to be a mistake, all of it.

The detective started speaking slowly then, making sure I didn't miss a single syllable.

Kristi. I'm going to tell you how your grandmother died last night.

I hated how he spoke about Betty—*the victim*—as if he had any right to talk about her like she was just some cold, dead body. Then he said something about her neck, or maybe he said throat.

Lacerations.

Signs of a struggle.

Bleeding out.

He told me about all the blood that had left her body after the weapon penetrated her skin over twenty times. I thought of how I hid under the blanket on my bed, while she screamed and screamed for help.

I'm burning.

I'm burning.

I'm burning.

Again: there was no fire.

When he started using the word *homicide,* I wondered what would happen if I threw something at the window behind him. Would it shatter into tiny pieces or just bounce back off the glass? People did that sometimes on TV. They got fed up with being questioned, being accused, when they just wanted someone to listen, really listen, to them. But he wouldn't shut up. He talked about the blood, how it had stained Mom's shirt in a way that meant she was the one holding the knife, the blade, whatever it was. They still hadn't found it. They thought I might know where it was, where Mom must have stashed it.

At one point, they even said it could have been one of the pens Betty kept near her bed.

You get angry enough, started one of the officers before he trailed off. I thought about it for a moment, about killing a person with a pen, and then, I had to stop. Instead, I wondered why she kept pens next to her bed—to write notes in the margins of the novels she read before she fell asleep? I'd never know now.

All day, the officers had been speaking about all of us in the past tense. When they asked me questions about Mom, it was *did she ever* and *had she ever* and *was she ever*. Mom was the suspect, Betty was the victim, and Nick and I were the witnesses. Our names, our home, the life we'd lived together didn't matter anymore. The family that the four of us had become would never exist in the present tense again.

Nick and I had been in police custody for hours when we learned that we had no place to go. I never thought it was possible to be so exhausted, drained of every ounce of energy. Since our house was a crime scene, we wouldn't be allowed to enter for twenty-four hours. Even our computer was turned over as evidence because of the Google searches about *how to kill.* At the station, all the rooms and cubicles were starting to clear out now, as if this were just a regular office where employees returned to their lives when it was finally 5:00 p.m.

After we were finished at the police station, we would be released to stay the night in town at the casino hotel alone since Nick was eighteen and I was still a minor. We were going to sleep at the casino where Betty used to work, where everyone knew us, alone, without either of our guardians.

What about Mom? I wondered, but I stayed quiet.

This wasn't how I thought it would be. I thought the police were supposed to dedicate their lives to helping people like they did on *SVU,* but they had worked on the case that day and clocked out just like Nick did at the end of his shifts at the supermarket after school. It didn't make sense. I wanted every officer and detective to put their lives on hold, to go back inside our house with their flashlights again and look harder, ask the right questions, try to find out *why.*

One of the cops said he can get us McDonald's breakfast, Nick said when the officers finally let us sit together. He was forcing a half smile, trying to give me some good news. We didn't acknowledge anything that had happened: the fact that we were in a police station, the fact that Betty was dead. Killed. I told him I wasn't hungry, but he was going to get in the car with the officer again anyway. Only one of us was allowed to leave the station.

Hotcakes with syrup, right? Nick asked with a smirk, and I nodded, smiling for the first time all day. I sat alone in another office, another cubicle, while he was gone. I wondered where Mom was, what was going through her mind. When he finally walked in with a grease-stained bag and a bottle of orange juice, someone else took us to a break room where we could sit at a table and eat together.

I picked up the plastic knife at the bottom of the bag, running my finger along the tiny white serrated edge. This was the first time we'd had the chance to eat since dinner last night, before we went to bed and woke up to the screams. My stomach had been growling for hours, but I didn't feel hungry. I couldn't feel at all.

We hadn't even eaten dinner at home last night. Instead, Nick had invited me to an end-of-year pizza party for the math students he tutored at the middle school. Had something happened while we were gone? Some argument about money, about one of Mom's boyfriends?

Everything was fine last night, I'd been saying all day. But I couldn't be sure, not really. I had a school-appointed psychiatrist, Dr. Finch, who'd been seeing me since the seventh grade after Mom called the school and told them I was suicidal when she found a poem I'd hidden in my room. Wouldn't Dr. Finch want to be here with me now, I wondered. Would she be able to help us figure out what was going on? I didn't know her phone number or how to get in touch with her outside of school.

As Nick unwrapped his egg sandwich, I poured a packet of syrup over the pancakes he'd brought for me. I started trying to cut them into pieces, but I kept thinking *lacerations*. I kept thinking *bleeding out*. The two of us sat in silence for a long time as people in uniforms came in and out of the break room to put lunch bags in the refrigerator and refill their coffee cups.

I thought back to everything the officers had said to me since we got there, whenever that was.

Your mother said she shot her with a gun, one of them had said.

She told us God made her do it, said another.

She told us she wanted to apologize to her son, said the one with the tattoo. *But you know what? She never mentioned anything about you.*

Toward the end of the day, when the sun had already set, I learned I would have to give my clothes to the detectives. They said everything I was wearing at the scene was considered evidence in the case. There were two or three women who were going to take me to the room where I could change.

Once we have your clothes, we'll give you something else to wear. You'll give your prints, and then, you guys will finally be on your way home, one of them said. Nick had already changed out of his clothes before we left, leaving his bloodstained basketball shorts on the floor of his room.

Will I get this stuff back? These are my favorite shoes, I said, looking down at the checkered turquoise Vans that Nick had helped me pick out at the mall a few months earlier. Betty had given us some money to pull the weeds out of the gravel in our driveway one Saturday after it had rained. I was tired of asking questions. I was tired of the way the officers talked to me like I was nobody, like I didn't even matter to them. I didn't understand that I was being treated like someone who was guilty of something. That they weren't looking at me as a fifteen-year-old girl whose grandmother had just been killed and whose mom was suspected of committing the crime. That they only saw me as one of the three people who were present when one of their victims was murdered.

Nick was taken to a room to give his fingerprints, and I followed the women to another room with another one-way mirror. I was sick of seeing myself in those reflections, of being reminded of all my nights watching TV with Mom and Betty, egging Detective Benson on as she questioned suspects in her very own interrogation room. But I had never seen an episode where she asked anyone—let alone a teenage girl—to take off their clothes.

There was a table lined with brown paper, the kind I wrapped my textbooks with at the beginning of each school year. I asked if I should go into the bathroom to change and what I was supposed to wear after I was done. They told me I would have to change in the room, right there, with them. They said they would turn around, but the whole room was a mirror, so I knew they'd see me anyway.

One woman instructed me to take off each article of clothing and place it on top of the brown paper table to be touched only by gloved hands and placed in a bag labeled *Evidence*. Aside from doctors and family, no one had ever seen me naked before. The women kept looking, waiting, ready for me to start removing my clothes. I started feeling weak, knees shaking and fingers tingling.

I don't have any blood on my clothes, I thought, but I couldn't speak. Goosebumps crawled up my bare stomach toward my neck as I started to remove the shirt I'd worn to bed, before any of this had happened. Before I had any idea what a scream really sounded like. I could feel their eyes on me as I placed the shirt on the table, crossing my arms to keep them from seeing more of me. I reached for the pink drawstring tied in a bow around my waist, and for the first time all day, I started to cry.

I don't have any blood on my clothes. I don't. I don't. I promise I don't. My pants fell to the ground, and I could hear myself begging now, wanting to be left alone, trying to wrap myself up with my own trembling arms. I had never felt more alone, more exposed, more violated. Like I wasn't a person but a piece of evidence, a thing to be filed away and forgotten somewhere inside the station. I wished I could be invisible, something no one would ever have to look at again. It felt like a dream, some kind of living nightmare, just a rerun left playing in some empty bedroom overnight.

After everything I was wearing at the scene was finally on the table, then in the bag, one of the women handed me a large blue jumpsuit to wear.

It's one size fits all. I tried not to cry again while I slipped my feet into the light blue paper booties that came with it. I could barely breathe. I tried to hold the loose pants up around my waist while someone new instructed me to do what Nick had just done: press my fingers into the black ink and roll the tips of my fingers and thumbs from left to right on a sheet of thin paper. All I could think of was sleep, how I'd never been so tired in my life.

You're helping our investigation by doing this, sweetie, said the detectives. *You're doing a great job.*

By the time Nick and I wiped the ink off our fingers, Mom had already been charged and was waiting to go to the county jail for the murder of her own mother.

On the way to the hotel, the officers asked us if we were hungry. Even though the last thing I'd eaten was a few bites of the McDonald's pancake all those hours ago, I couldn't imagine eating. They took us through the KFC drive-through while we listened to a top forty radio station. They ordered fried chicken with mashed potatoes and gravy, passing two plastic bags to the backseat without turning to look at us. As we drove back to our town with warm bags of food on our laps, the officer in the driver's seat turned up the radio as the pop song "Bleeding Love" played through the speakers.

I used to love that song, and I thought of how Nick and I would jokingly sing along in high-pitched voices as he drove us to school in the mornings. *You cut me open and I keep bleedin', keep keep bleedin' love.* This time, we didn't even look at each other. I sat in silence and thought again of the blood that had come from Betty's body. I shut my eyes, trying to turn off the image, hoping I could blink and make it go away forever.

I was embarrassed to walk through the hotel lobby in my jumpsuit, so Nick walked ahead of me in case anyone passed us in the hall. I thought of the time a boy I had a crush on from school saw me at the grocery store in sweatpants buying maxi pads, how I hid in the laundry detergent aisle with my cheeks burning red. I didn't want to imagine being seen in the jumpsuit by anyone other than Nick—it was worse than sweatpants or the pajamas I left at the police station or any other embarrassing outfit I'd ever worn. We pretended Nick's tall, thin body was enough to stop other people from seeing what I was wearing.

I thought the officers were going to stick around, but they left as soon as we swiped the card through the lock on the door. Suddenly Nick and I were all alone in a hotel room that smelled like cigarette smoke—the same way our house used to smell. I thought of Betty's pack-a-day, how I used to fear that someday smoking was going to kill her. I thought of the cigarette she kept pressed between her lips almost all the time. I thought of the smoke floating in the air above her as we watched *Jeopardy!* together every night, each of us trying to outsmart the other and both of us answering every question wrong. On those nights, we spent hours talking and laughing and yelling in our pajamas, and I sometimes wished that she was my real mother. I never told her that, and now, she was never going to know.

Nick and I placed our untouched KFC dinners on the hotel coffee table and turned on the TV in front of the bed. Maybe we thought it would be a distraction while we waited for Nick's friend and his mom to bring us some clothes to wear before we could go back into our house the next day. Would we want to go back in at all? The first thing that came up on the screen was a small adobe house with a turquoise door and four matching pillars crossed off with yellow caution tape. It took me a moment to realize what we were looking at. I could almost see the window to my room, but Betty's silver Jeep was blocking it. I stared at the front license plate we'd gotten custom-made for her at the mall: *B e t t y* spelled out in cursive letters across a green background with five playing cards on the side.

Make sure it's a royal flush, Mom had said to the woman working at the kiosk.

In the top right corner of the television screen, I saw her: tired in her own jumpsuit, holding up a card that said her name and a list of numbers I didn't understand. Below it were the words *WOMAN STABS MOTHER 20 TIMES* floating across a blue banner. I looked down at the jumpsuit I would finally get to take off when the clothes got here, and I thought of how Mom would probably have to wake up still wearing hers tomorrow. I looked at Nick for what felt like the first time all day, and he held my hand while our mashed potatoes and gravy got cold on the table beside an ashtray.

It's all over the news, May said with tears in her eyes when she walked into the hotel room. We didn't tell her that we knew already, that we had seen Mom's face on the news when we got to the room. May lived down the street from us with her son, Tyler, and her daughter, Melinda, who both went to our school. Although Tyler was in the sophomore class with me, he and Nick, both with piercings on their faces and gauges in their ears, had become best friends through the hardcore bands they saw on the weekends. They broke into our high school together to throw eggs at all the windows and listened to loud music.

May handed me a stack of clothes in the doorway of the bathroom: a T-shirt, cotton shorts, and a pair of lime green underwear with a bow in the front that she'd found in her daughter's dresser. I wondered how long it would be until I could wear clothes from my own dresser. I wanted to know if there were still police officers in the house, going through my things, deciding what was suspicious enough to go into their bags and what could be left behind.

I closed the bathroom door and looked at myself in the mirror one last time before I changed out of the jumpsuit. I turned the faucet on and let the water run as I stared at myself, steam climbing across the mirror, blurring my reflection. I saw my face again for the first time since the interrogation room—my dark blonde hair frizzy around my face from the moisture in the air, my eyes green like Betty's used to be, tears streaming out and rolling down my cheeks.

In the shower, I leaned against the wall with the plastic curtain pushed open. Drops of water jumped out of the tub and pooled on the floor and I thought of the blood on the tile in Betty's room. Would everything remind me of that for the rest of my life? Somehow I thought that taking off the jumpsuit would make me feel better, but it only made me feel worse, like the day was really over and there was no way to go back.

I wondered if Mom was going to go to jail. I wondered what would happen to her there, how long she would be gone. I wondered how much of my life she was going to miss now, who I was going to become without her or Betty. I wondered what was going to happen to Betty's house. I wondered, too, as I would for a long time, why Betty had been killed while the rest of us had not. There was still one question that I was too afraid to ask: did Mom really murder Betty? While the two of us were sleeping down the hall? I thought of all the things the detectives had told me about her at the station.

We found a whole lot of prescription pill bottles in your mother's room, one of them had said. I didn't tell the officers that I already knew about the collection of orange bottles on her bedside table, how the pills could turn her into somebody I couldn't recognize, like the unfamiliar names printed on their labels. I didn't tell them about my classmate's summer birthday party where one of the other moms pulled me aside as I licked icing off the corner of my lip.

Sweetheart, she said, holding a plastic cup filled with lemonade. *I think your mom has a problem. She buys prescription drugs from these illegal websites.* I knew she took Klonopin, relied on it. She'd been taking it since she was nineteen, when she was first diagnosed with panic attacks. I could feel my stomach sinking as I stared down at the piece of yellow cake on my paper plate.

Everyone always thought Mom was interesting, a little *off.* She didn't act like other moms. She acted more like one of us, a teenager trapped in a forty-four-year-old woman's body. She had a Myspace profile she made me take pictures of her for, wearing heavy makeup and trendy clothes. She would try to get me to wear more revealing clothes and more makeup like her, saying things like, *When you're my age, you're going to wish you hadn't wasted it.* As one of her many jobs, she had worked as a teacher's aide once in the special education department at our high school for a while, and the boys in my classes would say, *Your mom is so much hotter than you.* She would wear clothes she took out of the drawers of my dresser, squeeze into my jeans, and then, sixteen-year-old boys hit on her in the halls while Nick and I were in our classes nearby. I wondered what the people at school were going to say about her now when they saw her face on the local news.

I had been in the shower so long now that the pressure of the water left a patch of red across my chest. As I rinsed my hair, I wondered how many pills had been swimming around inside Mom when Betty died. I didn't want to get out, to have to face Tyler and his mom when I knew that after they left, they would have to drive past our house and see the yellow caution tape. I thought it would feel good to take a shower, to lather and scrub and rinse off everything that had happened that day, to watch it run through the holes in the rusty drain. But all I wanted was to hold onto it, to be who I was the day before when Betty was still alive and Mom wasn't charged with murder. I dried off and turned the fan on, making sure I put Melinda's clothes on before the steam cleared up enough to show my whole reflection. I didn't want to look at my naked body in a mirror ever again; it would only remind me of the three officers who wrapped my clothes up and called them evidence.

Rio Grande Sun
May 15, 2008

Chilling Account of Nambé Woman's Murder

Kristi D. awoke in the middle of the night May 6 to the sounds of her grandmother screaming.

She looked at her bedroom clock: 1:58 a.m.

"Help me. Help me," her 68-year-old grandmother yelled.

The 16-year-old [*sic*] got out of bed but was too afraid to leave her room. She knew all the doors and windows were locked in the Nambé house she shared with her grandmother, mother, and 18-year-old brother; there had been a rash of car break-ins recently and a few weeks ago a stranger had knocked late at night on a neighbor's door, so the family was being careful. Besides, she hadn't heard the dogs bark.

But nevertheless, the noises she heard were the sounds of her grandmother being attacked.

So she stood there, in her white Hello Kitty pajamas, listening to her grandmother and waiting for the sound of her mother's footsteps to run down the hall to her grandmother's aid.

But those footsteps never came.

There were full-sized beds for Nick and me in the hotel room, but for some reason, we decided to pull the folded mattress out of the couch instead. We lay down next to each other with all the lights in the hotel room still on. The last thing I remembered was him holding my hand, the two of us side by side staring at the ceiling. In the morning, Nick was still right beside me, wide-awake, face up. Did he ever fall asleep that night? I wanted to ask how he was doing, what he was thinking about, if he felt how I felt, but I couldn't.

We didn't know what was going to happen to us or how to talk about what already had. Nick said we would probably move to Florida to live with our dad and stepmom, Val. We had been in touch with them again, and Mom had even threatened to ship me off to live with them when she found my hidden poem and told the school principal I was a danger to myself. Nick was already planning to go there after graduation, enroll in a college nearby so he could spend time with Dad after being apart over the years. He always said he couldn't wait to get out of here, get away from Mom.

Was Nick still going to go to college at all? He would graduate in two weeks, and neither Betty nor Mom would be there to watch. He tried to pretend nothing was wrong, to make me feel safe and comfortable, and told me it was going to be okay. He had been doing this all my life, challenging me to *Goldeneye* on Nintendo 64 to distract me from the chaos of our childhood with Mom. Now, there was nothing we could do to escape how real this was.

Let's play James Bond *again,* I used to beg when I could sense him getting tired or bored of spending time with me. I always wanted him to play long enough for me to fall asleep before I had the chance to wonder if Mom was going to come home soon from another night out.

I didn't know where she went when she left us at the house alone, but maybe Nick did. We didn't talk about that. We only talked about Gameboy and Stone Cold Steve Austin and how we were going to use the plastic trash can lid as a sled when we finally got to see the snow. We both had blonde hair and big teeth like Dad, and sometimes, people asked us if we were twins. I always wanted to say yes even though I knew it was a lie. I had no memories of Dad and Mom in the same room together. In my mind, it was almost as if they had never been married at all. I couldn't remember much, but I knew there were good times with Dad, when we did fun things like rollerblade down the hallway of his apartment building or drink chocolate milkshakes in the back of his car while Nirvana played on the radio.

Whenever Mom was gone again, I tried to think of it as a night with Nick instead of one without Mom, like I learned to do with Betty later. I woke up some nights just to make sure that Nick was still there—sleeping on the bottom bunk, breathing my air, making me whole. I would climb halfway down the ladder or hang my head over the metal railings just to see if he was still with me. I wouldn't have been able to stand it if he was gone the way that Mom still was in the late hours of the night.

Now, in the hotel room, we were fifteen and eighteen, waiting for someone to save us. For a moment, I thought about Craig, our old stepdad who'd been out of our lives for over three years now—since we watched him leave in the middle of the night after a fight with Mom. I wondered what he would think if the news of her arrest reached him all the way in North Carolina. I sat up against the couch and tried to picture a life with Craig or even Dad, but I couldn't. The only life that made sense was the one we had with Betty. She loved us. She had made a home for us, gave us things we'd never had before.

I never attended class at my high school again, though I did go back once to return my textbooks and clear out my locker. In the halls, the other students stared at me, almost like I was some kind of celebrity. I had put on makeup, tried to look how I imagined a normal person would. Blue eyeliner, a new thing I'd seen in one of Mom's fashion magazines a few weeks earlier. Sparkly eyeshadow. Sheer lip gloss. But I was not a normal person anymore, as that short walk through the halls confirmed.

People who didn't know me offered half smiles. Girls who'd disliked me, who'd made fun of me in the past, ran up to me. Threw their arms around me. Reminded me to call them, reach out any time, even though

I didn't have any of their phone numbers. My old science teacher walked by, but he didn't try to approach. He held his hand up in front of his face, as if to say, *Don't.* When he was almost out of earshot, he said, *My heart goes out.*

I always wondered why, what that meant. Did he feel bad about not stopping? Does he ever think about it now? He'd meant a lot to me once, in the way that teachers mean a lot to students with dysfunctional home lives. When he introduced the class to the movie *Contact* starring Jodie Foster the year before, I became obsessed with it, even stayed after class to talk to him about it.

What kind of college do you need to do what Jodie did in the movie? I asked, excited. But I had no plans to attend college, really. How could I leave, make plans of my own, when Mom was at home, sleeping half the day? When I got back to the hotel after the trip to my locker, I was shocked: I'd never had so many Myspace friend requests in my life.

My English teacher, Mrs. Ortiz, visited us at the hotel with some extra clothes and a plastic container of leftovers. Dad was there with us, helping make arrangements with some of Betty's other family members. She asked to speak to me alone. People from school and the casino had been coming in and out of the hotel to check in on us, even some we didn't know. It was nice enough, but it was exhausting, too. Another person to smile for, to thank for coming over. Another person to ask how we were holding up, if there was anything they could do to help. In the parking lot, with tears welling up in her eyes, Mrs. Ortiz told me she felt guilty.

I ignored your cry for help, she said. *You reached out to me and I ignored you. Remember?* I tried to pretend I didn't know what she was talking about. A few months earlier, the school had sent out information packets about registering for classes for the following year, and when Mrs. Ortiz put one on my desk, I said I didn't need it.

I don't know if I'll be here anymore, I said. *My mom is being kind of crazy.* But I didn't mean it like that. I meant that Nick was going to move to Florida to go to college anyway, and I'd thought about going with him, getting out of here. Even though I hated the idea of leaving Betty, I was planning to follow Nick because I didn't want to be left alone to take care of Mom while he was gone. Mrs. Ortiz laughed and said, *Well, we'll miss ya!* before she handed the registration forms to another student.

You told me something was wrong, she said. *Maybe I could have . . .* and then she trailed off, looking out at the cars in the hotel parking lot. I told her I didn't even remember saying that. I told her it must have been someone else. I told her not to feel bad, that there was nothing any of us could have done to change *what happened*. I had spent the last week hearing the same thing from other people. I couldn't understand why it was my responsibility to make *them* feel better. I was the one who was hurting. I was the one who couldn't sleep or think or get through the day without hearing those screams.

That night, I lay down beside Nick in a gray sweatshirt that Mrs. Ortiz had given us in a bag full of clothes. I kept trying to replay our conversation about the paperwork, wanting to hear myself say, *My mom is being kind of crazy*. I thought it over and over again. *My mom is being kind of crazy. My mom is being kind of crazy*. I hadn't said it in a private meeting with Mrs. Ortiz or a friend or the guidance counselor. I'd said it in class loud enough for my classmates to hear it, and now, I kept asking myself if it was true. What did it even mean? Did I want someone to do something about it? Maybe they thought I was kidding then. Maybe I thought I was kidding, too. But part of me wondered now if it really was a cry for help. Would anything have happened differently if someone had listened? Would Mom have ended up somewhere other than the jail cell she was in now, as if that was supposed to make any of this better?

Soon after Mrs. Ortiz's visit, some family members got together at the top of a dusty hill to scatter Betty's ashes. They'd flown in from across the country, grief-stricken and horrified. We found a quiet spot not far from our house off a desert trail. Everyone took turns speaking out loud to her, saying things they wished they had said when she was still alive. I was the only one who didn't say anything. I couldn't. I didn't know how.

As I listened to everyone speak, I wondered how it could be a funeral if there was no body to bury. I watched Nick, in a light blue button-down shirt, fall to his knees as he spoke. I felt helpless seeing him cry, really cry, for the first time in my life. I tried to picture Betty in one of her nightgowns or maybe in a vest with one of her rhinestone shirts. All I wanted was to see her the way I used to, but I could only see my brother's grief and the blood on Mom's shirt.

PART TWO Before/After

In the dreams, Betty was almost always dead. She never had a face, never spoke words other than the bad ones like *no* and *help* and *burning*. She used to say more than that, *be* more than that, though it was hard to remember. She used to tell me jokes and talk about her favorite books, and I was certain she had a laugh that was all her own. When she was alive, she was *something else*, as people around town said. Not the way Mom had been, how people called Mom *not all there* or *a little off* or *really pretty but sort of strange.*

I was mesmerized when we first moved into Betty's old house on the corner of a narrow dirt road. It wasn't *the* house, or the one before that, but the one before that. She had lived there with her husband, the last of many—at least four, I'd been told. He'd died of cancer some time before. The first day I spent time with her alone, I sat across from her on the peach-colored leather couch in her living room while she smoked a cigarette. I must have been ten years old then, getting ready to start the fifth grade at the local school. Nick had spent time with her when he was younger, but I couldn't remember if I had. She told me she was a witch, that she could put a curse on anyone who crossed her. She told me stories while her Chihuahuas scratched at the sliding glass door beneath a row of bright red strawberry-shaped hummingbird feeders.

It was the height of summer, and it had to be almost ninety degrees outside, but she was wearing a corduroy vest with a red long-sleeve shirt underneath.

Aren't you hot under all those clothes? I asked, wiping sweat off my forehead. In the middle of her shirt was a silver shooting star made of plastic rhinestones that fit perfectly between the two panels of the vest. I would soon learn that she wore a version of this outfit every day, like she was some cartoon character whose closet consisted of a row of hangers all holding the same outfit.

Hey, Kris, she said, calling me a name no one else had ever called me before. *Want to make yourself useful and help me do something important?* She didn't seem like she could be anybody's grandmother. She cursed more than anyone I'd ever met, even more than Mom or the other adults I'd known. She cursed so much it made me turn red, big blotches crawling up my bony neck. She went into the other room and came out again with her ironing board under one arm and a stack of long-sleeve shirts in the other.

What are we doing? I asked.

Bedazzling some shit, she answered. She pulled out a plastic bag full of iron-on rhinestone patterns like the one on her shirt.

At 7:25 a.m. the day after the murder, the local news station reported her death between stories about a doomsday cult and a University of New Mexico student who was found with guns in his dorm:

> Sixty-eight-year-old Betty R. was found dead yesterday morning in the home she shared with her daughter and her two grandchildren. Her throat had been cut.

In the beginning, before all of that, there was Craig, our stepdad. Before the divorce, before the yelling and the crying and the moving in with Betty, he would smile at Mom while they danced to "Hotel California" in the middle of the kitchen and took drags from their respective cigarettes. He'd put one hand on the small of her back and wink at me from across the room, singing the lyrics into her ear while I sat on the countertop beside the growing supply of glass bottles: blue for vodka, green for wine, clear for whiskey. I was just a kid then, excited that someone was around who had convinced Mom to stay awake in the daytime. But that was before everything *went to shit,* as Betty would later call it. It didn't take long for me to notice each bottle on the counter getting emptier and emptier, faster and faster.

Later, after my nineteenth birthday, four years after the murder, Craig called me. He said, *I should have been there. I should have been with you guys. Then it wouldn't have happened. There wouldn't have been a murder.* Most of the adults—estranged family members, distant family friends—would say something like that eventually.

Some days, when Mom and I were alone, she'd talk to me like I was a grown-up about things I wouldn't understand until I became one. Mostly, she'd tell me how much she wanted to die.

I don't want you to find me, she'd say. *I can't do it in the house.* By the time I was old enough to know what it meant, I'd already lost track of how many times she said it. Sometimes it got so bad she'd sit Nick and me down in the kitchen and tell us how she wanted to lie down on the street in the middle of traffic. But we always knew she had a gun in her room because that was how she proved to us she could really do it. If she wanted to, she assured us, she could really kill herself. It wouldn't be that hard.

Soon, though, Nick stopped listening. He practically moved into his best friend Ryan's house down the street while I was Mom's captive audience. There were times she told me she'd drive out somewhere far from home and do it in the car. Other times, she said she'd stand in the middle of a forest where no one could hear the bullet leave the barrel. She always said she was going to wear a lot of makeup the day she finally died, so, when they found her, wherever she was, she would still have her beauty.

Whenever she told us she was going to do it, I would picture her in a field, someplace pretty with daisies or tulips or wildflowers. She'd hold the black handgun up to her head with black Maybelline tears rolling down her cheeks. Or maybe she wouldn't cry at all. Her manicured finger would pull the trigger, and in an instant, my only mother would be gone. The petals in the field would be stained now, redder than the collection of lipsticks Mom lined up in the medicine cabinet above the sink in the bathroom.

Just a kid, I couldn't understand how someone so glamorous could be so sad. She was everything I wanted to be when I grew up, and ever since I could remember, men would come up to her while she was pumping gas or loading plastic bags into the back of the car just to ask if she was really my mother.

You must be sisters, they'd say, eager and smiling. *You look too young to be her mother.* She was the most beautiful person I'd ever seen, and I was proud that she was my mom. I loved to watch her put her makeup on, mixing two or even three shades of foundation on the back of her hand to match her skin tone perfectly. She was always doing *something* while she looked in the mirror—exfoliating or moisturizing or dabbing cotton balls in olive oil to prevent wrinkles around her eyes and mouth.

Her hair and nails seemed to change color weekly, but she never got them done professionally. I'd forgotten how many times I'd seen her open a box of drugstore dye and slide the clear plastic gloves over the shiny nails she filed and painted on a stack of fashion magazines on her bed. Her hair was always different, as she switched from light to dark and back again more times than I could count. She always seemed to be chopping it off, too, claiming the damage she'd done to the ends with bottles of extra strength bleach and boxed dyes could never be repaired.

Getting a trim helps it grow faster, she'd say, though it never seemed to make it past her shoulders anymore.

Soon, it wasn't just her appearance that was changing, but the inside of our house, too. Craig, Nick, and I came home from school and work some afternoons to find that all the rooms in the house had been rearranged. Beds and dressers had been moved around. Our sheets and pillowcases were different. The microwave and the toaster were in each other's places. The forks were now where the spoons used to be. Some of our belongings were boxed up and taken away. Craig would complain that the glass or plate he wanted to use was missing, and they'd get in arguments about how Mom was never happy with anything.

We're going to Betty's, Mom said, one night after I heard Craig call her *fucking crazy,* pack his yellow duffle bag, and get into his truck and disappear. Neighbors had been complaining about their fights. Police had been coming to the house. Rooms had been trashed. Bottles had been broken. Mom hadn't been eating. Nobody made dinner; nobody said goodnight.

One night, Mom's friend from one of her old jobs came over and tried to distract me from the screaming and crying Mom and Craig were doing on the lawn. She microwaved a frozen corn dog for me, tried to make conversation while I picked at it, telling her I hated mustard. I couldn't remember ever being so hungry. When it was time to go to Betty's, we got rid of most of our things at a garage sale, setting up old dishes and clothes perfectly on the lawn. I hugged my friends from the soccer team, Nick said bye to Ryan, and we got on a plane. Craig stayed behind.

Soon after we moved in, Betty and I developed a kind of relationship I'd never had with an adult before. Even though Mom lived with us, too, Betty became almost like another mother to me. She'd take me all the way to Santa Fe, to the mall and to restaurants where she'd convince me to try foods whose names I couldn't pronounce, had never even heard of before. We'd drive in her Jeep with the windows down, listening to one of the cassette tapes she kept in the backseat.

Her favorite kind of music was opera, but there were a few old pop and rock tapes hidden at the bottom of her collection, like *The Best of Carly Simon*. I loved to rewind the tape deck just to listen to "You're So Vain" again. I'd wonder later, though I didn't at the time, who she thought of when that song came on. Who did Betty think was vain? It's the kind of question you can only ask when you're older, when you know more than you did as a kid.

During our drives, when we weren't singing out of tune while Betty blew smoke out the window, we talked about books. On some Saturdays, we spent hours at Borders, Betty in the mystery section stocking up on James Patterson novels about murders in small towns and me carrying the list of titles she wrote down for me, like *The Outsiders* and *Heidi*. I could do things I couldn't do around Mom, like replay a song five times or read books for adults or talk about Ponyboy Curtis as if he were someone we both knew in real life.

Mom and I weren't getting along very well, even though I told people she was my best friend, that I had the coolest mom in the world. Her mood was always unpredictable: some days she'd invite me to the mall to buy me clothes, shower me with gifts, then the next day I'd come home from school to find she'd taken them out of my room and returned them. She'd tell me I was beautiful sometimes, that she loved the color of my eyes. Other times, she'd ignore me completely, walk past me as if I wasn't even there.

Around Mom, I almost always felt wary, nervous. Always afraid to do or say the wrong thing in case it would make everything worse, make her want to kill herself. That year, I learned what suicide really meant when a middle schooler who went to the after-school program with Nick and me at the Boys and Girls Club hanged herself in her bedroom one afternoon. When I realized she was really gone, never coming back, I feared more and more what Mom might do if she got sad enough.

Nick made friends with a boy named Forrest who lived down the road. He was no Ryan, but he lived in a house with a big swing and a trampoline and a brand-new GameCube. Sometimes we all rode our bikes together, but it was mostly me trying to keep up with them. They built a secret clubhouse in a big tree on the edge of the arroyo across from our house on a dirt road littered with dented cans of Tecate.

When he wasn't with Forrest or playing Yu-Gi-Oh, Nick would come along with Betty and me on some of our day trips to Santa Fe. We'd all pile into the Jeep to eat French food at an old hotel in the plaza or thumb through crates of old albums and trading cards at the flea market. I enjoyed living with Betty that year, becoming *Kris,* a kid who read books before bed every night, watched taped episodes of *Antiques Roadshow* on the weekends.

But it wasn't long before Mom came out of her room with news.

Craig's coming back, she said. We would all live here for a while, and then we'd move back to North Carolina at the end of the school year.

You'll start sixth grade back with your old friends at your old school. Mom and Craig would be back together, Nick would go back to spending all his time with Ryan and his parents, and I just wanted to ask, *Can Betty come with us, too?*

It was just the two of us this time—Mom and me driving in the green Mustang that Craig had helped her pick out. It was a convertible, but we couldn't put the top down, because the boxes were stacked so high that the black cloth above us had started to stretch over their cardboard corners. Some of our belongings were broken from how many times we'd moved already, driving from east to west and back again, but we kept some of them anyway. This time, finally, we were going back to New Mexico, to live with Betty again after almost a year.

North Carolina hadn't worked out. We had picked up and moved to Florida after just four months of living there. Now Florida hadn't worked out either. Nothing ever seemed to work out. And there was, as Mom put it, *no more fucking money*. I didn't have the reunion Mom promised with my old friends: we were getting older now, and things had changed while I was gone. Everyone had split up, moved on, started playing on new sports teams or acting at the local theater.

In Florida, Craig was working as a car salesman while Mom was always quitting her latest job almost as quickly as she had started. Now, we were living on food stamps and welfare and disability checks. Our new home was supposed to give us a sense of stability, a place to land. I hated it. Trying to make friends in a small town where everyone had been in the same class together since kindergarten was impossible.

When the teacher introduced me as a new student from North Carolina, the other kids called me a hick, a redneck, a hillbilly, asking me if I'd ever heard of a thing called incest. When I explained I wasn't even from there, that I had lived in New Mexico before, too, they started asking me if I even understood English. It was the loneliest year of my life. Nobody wanted to be friends with the new girl. Nobody wanted to *be* the new girl three times in a single school year.

Without Betty buying us groceries and clothes for school that year, we were the poorest we'd ever been. My nickname at school was Highwaters because all my pants were too short for my growing body. Hardly any of my clothes fit, and the ones that did were from thrift stores with childish patterns or catchphrases on them like *Lucky Duck, Princess Alert,* or *You Go Girl!* Most of the boys were already bragging about making out, and the girls were wearing crop tops to show off their homemade safety pin belly button piercings. I felt like I'd somehow missed a step of growing up, like I was still just a little kid while my classmates were becoming teenagers, almost adults, right in front of me. I'd beg Mom to let me stay home from school all the time. I'd rather sit on the couch watching daytime game shows while she napped all day than have to walk to class with my head down and eat lunch alone again.

I thought, I should tell someone about this. But I didn't want Mom to know, didn't want her to think I was a burden. She was reactive, erratic. I never knew what to expect when I'd come home from school. Sometimes she'd be boxing up everything we owned; other times she'd be hanging up new Martha Stewart curtains she just bought at Kmart. I started to wonder if she was, in the words of our neighbor who pulled me aside one afternoon, *not all there.* I didn't want to do anything that would push her over the edge, make her want to kill herself.

When Mom said we would be moving back to Betty's soon—that we wouldn't even have to wait till the end of the school year—I was relieved, excited, for the first time in so long. Finally, a good thing. I'd lived in two other states since the last time I saw Betty. While we were gone, living out of boxes, she had moved into a new house in another town north of the old place we shared. It was bigger with three bedrooms and a big yard with fruit trees I didn't even know could grow in a place as dry as New Mexico. I wondered if she knew when we left the first time that we'd be coming back. This time, the house would be big enough for Nick and me to have our own rooms. Mom and Craig would have to live in the garage after they fixed it up with a new door and a couple of coats of paint.

By then, we hadn't talked to our real dad in years, but I wondered about him often. I used to write him letters, put them in the mailbox addressed to a place I knew he'd lived before in Miami. I never heard back, assumed he didn't care to talk to me.

Is there something wrong with me? I'd ask in bright blue gel pen. It was years later that I'd find out Mom walked out to the end of the driveway at night and took the letters out. Opened them, read the private things I wrote, like, *I hate it here. I'm not happy. Are you?* I never knew if she threw them away or kept them, but she'd console me sometimes when I'd cry myself to sleep because my dad didn't want me.

Craig was going to be coming along to our new house with Nick in a few weeks because Nick wanted to finish out his eighth-grade school year *in one place.* Although I missed him, I envied his insistence. I wished I could be like that. Make my own decisions. The drives each day on the way back to Betty's were so long it felt like I hadn't seen Nick in forever, but there was a photo of us wearing Power Rangers Halloween costumes wrinkled in the glove box. I liked to look at his face under the glow of lights along the interstate as we drove away from our old life.

Some of Mom's vintage China had cracked and chipped at the bottom of a box labeled *kitchen* without the letter T. I'd spelled it wrong with my blue marker—the only one left in the pack from the last time Mom took us school supplies shopping. At that age, I hated school and everything about it. I no longer enjoyed reading like I used to when we lived with Betty, when she'd take me to Borders and fun restaurants. I didn't have any of the books she'd bought me anymore except for *The Outsiders*. I hadn't picked it up in months. I stopped getting attached to material objects, knowing I'd probably move again soon and lose special things, the stuff that mattered to me. I didn't feel curious anymore, didn't care to learn anything new.

Most mornings, I'd tell Mom and Craig I had stomachaches, which wasn't even really a lie. When I did go to school, I'd call Mom at lunch and ask her to pick me up. I liked when she would come get me and take me places, like to stand in line with her at some government office to argue with some apathetic person behind a counter. When she finally got the money she was after, she spent it on fast food and orange bottles of pills that she would line up beside her bed.

Sometimes her voice sounded different after she'd put her head back to swallow a handful of capsules with a to-go cup of coffee. Only when she was desperate, she drank it black like the mascara she used to paint her eyelashes, to make them look longer and younger. I heard her voice change and feared that maybe she was trying to *become* someone else, so reliant was she on the tranquilizers she kept in her purse.

Now, the bottles were scattered on the floor of the car beneath my feet, next to the Sarah McLachlan CD we'd listened to for three days straight. On good days, we'd smile with the windows down and sing, *I will remember you. Will you remember me?* Or we'd listen to the radio and argue about the lyrics of "Drops of Jupiter" every time it came on. Sometimes I felt like

I never wanted it to end. Other times I couldn't wait to get out of that car, finally get away from her and have a moment alone.

When Mom, Nick, and I moved to New Mexico to live with Betty the first time, Mom had started gambling with what money she had. She spent more and more time at the casino where Betty worked. The two of them would sit next to each other pushing buttons, collecting tokens, and getting free food from the buffet. While we drove from our old home to our new home, Mom and I made a game out of looking for gas stations with slot machines inside, and when no one was looking, she would let me pull the lever with fingers stained from a brand-new bag of Cheetos.

On the road, we ate McDonald's apple pies every night because they were two for a dollar, and we'd take them in the motel rooms where Mom would stand on the bed and disconnect the smoke detector if we couldn't get a smoking room. As we ate, she'd tell me her grown-up problems, and I'd nod along, trying to be supportive.

I don't have an identity, she'd say. *I don't have a self. I never did and I never will.* Then she'd lie in the dirty bathtub with a cigarette between her lips, ashes swimming with the bubbles as mascara stained her cheeks. I wore pajamas on our long drives, gray sweatpants that Nick had outgrown a few years earlier, and when I asked Mom why she still took the time to put on all that makeup, she'd say, *You never know who you might see. Besides, my looks are all I have.*

Our house in Florida had been the first place since Betty's that we had cable. In the few months we lived there, I spent most of my time alone watching TV. I didn't have any friends at school, and as always, Nick had found a friend whose family let him sleep over all the time. I'd sit on the floor among the still-packed moving boxes, flipping through the channels, stumbling across shows like *America's Most Wanted* or *Unsolved Mysteries.* I was intrigued by the fascinating and disturbing stories, mostly of children my age who went missing all across the country.

Not long before Mom told me we were leaving to move back in with Betty, my elementary school went on lockdown. A fifth-grade girl reported that a man had attempted to kidnap her outside of one of the bathrooms on our campus. I didn't know the girl, but everyone knew who she was after it happened, and everyone had an opinion about the allegations. Some said she made it up to get attention, others said they were glad she got away from the man who tried to grab her. She told the police he was wearing a suit and tie with no shoes on, and a black-and-white drawing of his face was posted up all over town. It was like the images I'd seen on *America's Most Wanted* each night: his shadowy eyes haunted me, following me in the hallways at school, revealing a darkness that made me fearful, uncomfortable.

Less than a month earlier, an eleven-year-old girl named Carlie Brucia had been abducted, raped, and killed just two hours away from our small town. The case garnered statewide attention after the abduction was captured on a security camera outside the carwash where Carlie was last seen. In the days and weeks that followed, local news stations seemed to play the video constantly, and soon, it made national news, too. Even after Carlie's body was found and the man in the video was arrested, it felt like that image was all we ever saw each time we turned on the TV. First, the message was, *Help us find this man.* Then, it became, *Be afraid: there are more like him.* The video was burned into my mind, impossible to forget. In it, a blurry young Carlie wears a red shirt as a man grabs her arm and takes her away.

Kids at school talked about the case all the time, saying their parents were being strict now because they were afraid. Throughout it all, I found myself sad—almost irrationally—as if I had any right to grieve for some girl I'd never known. I just felt so bad for Carlie, who had been walking home from a sleepover when the man approached her. I felt sad for her family, for all the people in her life who had to go on living with that video replaying in their minds even after the news stations would move on to something new.

After the girl at my school said she ran away from the man in the suit, my sadness turned to guilt. Now, I felt like a bad person for having watched these shows about all the missing kids. They were real. Their suffering was real. I wondered what was wrong with me for finding it *interesting*. During that drive from Florida back to New Mexico with Mom, I recognized the names of some cities and towns from the *America's Most Wanted* episodes I'd seen, places where innocent kids had vanished. A fear grew in me. It seemed every new place could be tainted by some evil, some bad thing that could happen in an instant.

The first thing I saw when I went back to town was the casino. It was daytime, so the parking lot was less crowded, but I missed seeing Betty's Jeep in the first row. It had been three months since she died. I missed knowing she was inside the poker room, laughing in a cloud of smoke as she dealt cards in one of her vests. Passing through town, I saw the taco shop where she made me taste avocados for the first time and the video store where we used to rent romantic comedies and adaptations of books we loved. The long, winding road that led to our neighborhood reminded me of riding in the passenger's seat of the Jeep after school. I thought of how Betty would push the black button beneath the radio to heat up the car lighter and press it against the end of her cigarette as she held the wheel with one hand.

All the other houses, yards, and mailboxes looked the way they always had, but everything felt different. Once I saw my house, I wasn't thinking about car rides with Betty anymore; I could only remember how I felt in the back of the police car in the early hours of the morning she was killed. I thought of the black vinyl against my face as I lay down on the seat waiting to find out what happened to Betty, why Mom's hands were handcuffed behind her in the front yard. When we pulled up to the house, I saw that the weeds had overtaken the gravel and the tiny lanterns Nick had installed for Betty in the middle of the yard.

I still carried my house key with me every day since I left, wondering if I'd ever get to use it again. Now, in the driveway, I held it in my hands with the ring of colorful plastic charms I used to keep in my backpack. Except for the weeds, the house seemed the same from the outside, but it was hard to look at it without thinking of the last time I saw it. I knew the blood had been cleaned up months ago, but I was still afraid of what her room might look like in the daytime.

I couldn't bring myself to go to the front door yet, so I walked to the backyard instead, where I wanted to run my hands along the chain link fence Betty had paid Nick and his friends to build a couple of years earlier. But then I saw it: Betty's mattress leaning up against the side of the house, abandoned. It was covered in so much dry blood that it almost looked like there were light red sheets stretched over it.

Fuck, I said out loud, trying not to fall to my knees. There was nothing else to say. Somehow, I couldn't cry. It was like all those hours at the police station when I was so shocked that I couldn't feel anything.

I turned my key in the lock and pushed the door open. Inside, the air was still thick with cigarette smoke, and it was so hot it felt like the heater had been on all summer. The blinds had been left open for the last three months, and no one had ever come back into the house to close them. Even the blinds themselves were faded from the sunlight coming through. It made me wonder where Mom's and Betty's house keys had gone. Who was the last person to lock the door? Had Nick been carrying his key around all this time, too?

Everything was in the same place we'd left it in May before Nick and I moved to Florida to live with Dad. Betty's favorite piece of furniture was a round glass coffee table from the 1970s whose metal frame was painted metallic gold. She kept a handwritten address book on the table with a pack of cigarettes and a ceramic mug filled with pens and nail files. She collected Betty Boop memorabilia like lamps, key chains, and a giant blanket that Nick had hung up as the main decoration in the dining room. There were also tiny glass trinkets around the house that she collected—most were heart-shaped or flower-shaped or shiny things she had picked up while traveling. I didn't get to keep anything from the house except a small drawstring bag of pink and purple glass hearts she'd found on a trip by herself to some other city before I knew her.

I didn't want to look, but I couldn't keep my eyes away from the entrance to her room. Even with the sunlight shining through the blinds, I kept hearing Betty calling for help in the dark, waiting for me to come in and do something, anything. I couldn't that night and I couldn't now. The house looked like home, but it wasn't anymore. The four of us still had shoes lined up near the door, and there were still lipstick-stained cigarette butts in Mom's and Betty's respective ashtrays, but it felt like no one had ever lived here at all. Over the last three months, the house had become the version of itself I saw nightly in dreams: tragic, empty, and dark even in the daylight. It didn't feel like the same place where Betty and I had argued and laughed and cried together. It was something else now.

When I tried to walk into Betty's bedroom, I couldn't even make it past the doorway. The room was almost exactly the same except for the missing mattress. There were two bedside tables on either side of the empty bed frame, each one with a blue and red Betty Boop lamp on top. She bought them so she could read before bed, and sometimes, she'd stay up for hours just to finish an entire book in one night. Her collection of cacti sat yellowed and thirsty on the wrought iron shelf in the corner. On Sunday mornings, I used to lie in her bed as she watered them with a green can she kept in her room.

This one is my favorite, she'd told me about the one whose long arms spilled out from its pot. *It's called a rat tail.* I couldn't stand to look at it now, how lifeless it and everything else in the house had become without her. At least the last time I stood here, there was the possibility that everything was going to be okay because I didn't know yet that, by the following morning, the life I knew in that house with Betty, Nick, and Mom would never be the same again.

I wanted to see the rest of our rooms one last time. Mom's dresser had been searched and left open, socks and shirtsleeves dangling over the edges of the drawers. I imagined the police finding her gun there with their gloved hands as they looked for the real weapon that night and took notes on their clipboards. All of Nick's drawers and shelves had been rifled through, too, and only a few things had been left behind. I sat down on my bed and remembered Nick's arms around Mom and me as we waited for the police to come and get us. The last time the three of us were together. I wanted to know who would live there next, if this room would be an office or a bedroom or someplace someone could ever feel safe again.

All summer after the murder, I couldn't fall asleep with the lights off. Every time I was alone in the dark, I could see Betty there, lying motionless on the floor of her bedroom again. When I closed my eyes, it felt like I was standing in front of Mom, her hands red with blood as I tried to understand where all of it had come from. I slept in Nick's new room for a month before I could finally fall asleep by myself, but even then, the lights were on and the door was locked. The nightmares continued even when I had made enough progress that I could sleep alone. When I finally fell asleep, I always woke up in the middle of the night hearing the screams, seeing the blood. I'd run into Dad and Val's room every night around 2:00 a.m., convinced something bad was happening, so sure that they were hurt or dying. Two facts remained the same in both the nightmares and reality: Mom was always alive and Betty was always dead.

Everyone told me that someday the nightmares would turn to dreams and I would see Betty again the way I used to see her when she was alive, but I was already struggling to remember what she had been like. During the first few months, I realized how hard it would be to adjust to the world without her by my side. I was in a department store fitting room trying on clothes for my new school when "You're So Vain" started playing. I felt my body go numb, falling to the ground with only one of my arms through the sleeve of a shirt. The truth was that it was too hard to remember the good parts of her life—and of my life with her—because of how it ended.

At my new school, I was overwhelmed by the sheer size of the student body and the school grounds. My old high school in New Mexico had fewer than five hundred students in the entire student body, and my new school had over four thousand. I spent the first month of junior year trying to transition to the larger classes, crowded hallways, and smaller lockers. I never raised my hand or got called on to answer questions in class. I kept my head down, tried to hide. I didn't want anyone to ask me why I moved here, who I was. I had developed so many nervous habits: picking at the skin on my legs and arms, peeling off my nail polish in long strips even if I'd just painted it on the day before. I had to put on my bracelets and necklace in the same exact order each morning, convinced if I didn't, another bad thing would happen. I was ashamed of myself, didn't want to be seen. Every day, I ate lunch alone under two palm trees in the courtyard, and when the final bell rang, I walked home alone with my headphones on and waited to do it all over again the next day.

I wondered what college was like for Nick. I wanted to know if he was having as hard a time as I was, or if that was just normal for transitioning from high school to college. He was living in a dorm with three athletes who played on the university's baseball team together. He drove home almost every night to eat dinner with Dad, Val, and me even though they'd decided to spring for the meal plan so he could eat in the dining hall with the other students. Most nights, he slept at the house and woke up early to drive back in time for class, and the whole time, I wanted to ask if he was too scared to sleep in his own room at school.

I never saw the inside of his dorm, but I wondered what it looked like with the lights off, if its shadows took the shape of Mom's and Betty's bodies some nights like the ones I saw on the walls of my own new bedroom. I tried to tell Nick how much I was struggling in school to see if it would help him open up about how he was feeling, but he never did. I would never know about his dorm room or his schoolwork or if he missed Mom and Betty as much as I did. While Nick was at college, I had made it a point to remain as invisible as possible in my classes. It was junior year. Everyone was preparing for the SATs, getting ready to apply to college. I didn't know what I wanted to do with my life. I just wanted to sleep through the night.

Of all my new teachers, my history teacher, Ms. Graham, was the most intimidating. She wasn't like my old teachers in New Mexico. She gave the hardest tests, assigned the most homework, and bluntly called students out when they misbehaved. The walls of her classroom were covered in her alma mater's memorabilia and posters about equal rights. She wore mermaid earrings and painted her nails fun colors. My new classes were huge—some of them exceeded fifty students—and I was convinced Ms. Graham had never even seen my face. I didn't mind because I was afraid to get in trouble, to do the wrong thing.

My grades weren't good but not bad enough to catch any teacher's attention. She would walk through the aisles between our desks during quizzes to catch people reading answers off the insides of their fingers and embarrass them in front of the rest of us. She confiscated cell phones and bags of pills and pot, and she always seemed to be getting someone suspended or even expelled. The other students called her cruel names and made fun of her Southern accent behind her back.

Before Ms. Graham learned about Betty's murder, she confided in the class one morning about a tragedy in her own family in the '70s: a massacre at her family's farm in the rural South. The room was silent except for one of my classmates who seemed to think Ms. Graham might have been kidding and accidentally laughed out loud. Sometimes, people react in the strangest ways when you tell them something awful. They laugh, assume you must be joking. Things like that don't happen, they think. Not in real life. She sat on the edge of her desk and told us how the man, an escaped prisoner who'd orchestrated the crime, was executed on May 6 some years earlier.

I stopped listening then, frozen by how strange the date sounded coming out of her mouth. It had been so long since I'd heard anyone outside of my family say that date: the date that Betty was killed, the date that Mom was arrested, the date that broke our lives open. In my mind, the two words had become another way of saying *the murder*. I cringed when I heard it because it was more than a date now. It was strange to learn it had meant something else for Ms. Graham, too. She must have gone on to tell the class more about her family's story, but I was too stunned to hear her anymore. I felt connected to her somehow, even though she didn't know who I was.

Soon after, my new therapist, Dr. Elliot, who I'd been seeing every Wednesday after school, called the principal to tell him *what happened*. He told the guidance counselor, who told all six of my teachers that one of their students had witnessed a *brutal family tragedy* just months earlier. That's when all of them learned my name and started treating me differently.

Do you need to talk? they'd ask after class.

Everything okay at home? they'd write on scrap pieces of paper they'd leave on the corner of my desk.

I thought of you this weekend, they'd say, bringing me small gifts wrapped in discreet paper. I didn't know if any of the other students noticed that all of our teachers had started giving me, the new girl, a different kind of attention. I didn't want to feel guilty about it. I liked it. It was kind. It was validating.

My relationship with Ms. Graham began when she pulled me aside in class one morning.

We're going to be reading a violent book and then watching the movie adaptation, she said in a hushed voice. She told me I wouldn't have to read or watch if I didn't feel comfortable, that she would give me an alternative assignment. She didn't want the violence depicted to upset me, remind me of what I'd seen.

Thank you, was all I could muster, wiping away tears.

I had only told one person about the murder since I'd moved to Florida. Rachel lived in an apartment complex across the street from my house. We had met the week before school started, when Dad and I were shopping at Winn Dixie and saw her and a couple of boys walking through the parking lot. Dad went up to them and asked if they went to the local high school in an awkward attempt to help me make some friends. I was so embarrassed by him, worried that if these teenagers thought Dad was strange, I could only imagine what they'd say if they ever found out where Mom was.

But Rachel was kind. Before she and her friends left, she showed us her big, toothy smile and wrote down her house phone number on the corner of a piece of paper she'd ripped out of a notebook.

Call me! Let's have a sleepover! she said before we drove away. I was so grateful for Dad then I had to hold back tears. I sat staring at the numbers on the note and her name in curly blue letters: *Rach.* The whole summer I'd been nervous about making friends, rehearsing what I'd say if anyone asked me why I had moved here. I had lied a few times in the past when people asked me why I moved around so much.

Army brat, I said sometimes to curious classmates. It was an easy story to tell in the early 2000s, and most of the time people didn't ask any more questions.

I didn't want to lie to Rachel. She was going to become my new friend. My only friend. My best friend. We were going to have sleepovers every weekend and talk about boys and the new season of *Gossip Girl* and our periods. I would tell her about Mom, too, and she would understand. She would hold my hand and tell me it was going to be okay. She wouldn't just tell me she was sorry or that everything happens for a reason or that what doesn't kill me makes me stronger. She would know better than to use the word *kill* when we stayed up talking late at night. She would really be there for me, like a best friend was supposed to do. I pictured myself showing her Mom's letters, maybe even reading them aloud under string lights as we lay on my bedroom floor. Of course we were going to lie on my bedroom floor, I told myself. Soon, I wouldn't even miss my friends from my old school anymore.

Two days after I met Rachel, I finally dialed the phone number she had given me. I'd been keeping it in my pocket, waiting for the perfect amount of time to pass so she wouldn't find out how desperate I was to talk to someone, anyone, my own age.

How long had it been since I'd spoken to someone outside the house, other than a doctor or therapist? I didn't want her to know that I'd spent the last three months stuck at home with my nightmares, scratching my skin until I bled. I imagined what Rachel's summer must have been like so I could figure out what to make up in case she asked me about mine. I came up with a few lines about pool parties and movie marathons and practicing for my driving test. Calling Rachel was the only thing I could think about ever since I'd met her in the grocery store parking lot.

I kept imagining what I would say when I called and she picked up. I compared and contrasted the connotations of several greetings: *hey, hi, hello*, even *what's up*. Sounding cool *and* normal was my goal so I could convince Rachel to be my friend and get me out of my house. As much as I hoped she would invite me to sleep over at her house, I was afraid of waking up from a nightmare in front of her. What would she think when she heard me crying about the blood, trying to catch my breath? I told myself not to worry about it yet. She probably wouldn't ask me to spend the night right away. When I called her house phone, excited and nervous, it rang and rang before the operator said the number had been disconnected. I called back three times, and finally, I couldn't stop the sobs from coming.

Rachel had given me the wrong number on purpose. It was a prank. Was it because I needed my dad to help me make friends? I guessed that she wanted to seem nice in front of him, so she wrote down a fake number and assumed she'd never see us again. Dad insisted that it must have been a mistake.

Kids can't be that cruel, Val said at the dinner table. They both looked so disappointed, and I wondered if Dad felt responsible for Rachel's prank. I was convinced she must have somehow known about *what happened,* that she knew my mother was in jail for murder. That she would never be friends with someone like me. How could she have found out?

By the time school started, I thought I would never see Rachel again, especially since our school was so big, but one afternoon, there she was in the hallway wearing bright red skinny jeans with a cardboard sign hanging from her neck that read *Free Hugs!* I could feel my cheeks flush as soon as I saw her, and I tried to avoid eye contact and speed up on my way to class, but she chased after me.

Hey! Winn Dixie Girl! Remember me?

Oh. Hey, I said, embarrassed, but trying to pretend I didn't know who she was. I didn't know why she insisted on talking to me. I figured I could make her think I had never dialed the phone number in the first place.

I've been looking for you! she said. *I felt so bad because my mom forgot to pay the bill, so our phone was disconnected. I hope you didn't try to call!* She said she wanted to walk home with me after school since we lived so close to each other and hadn't gotten a chance to talk. I didn't know if I believed her about the phone number, but I was in no position to pass up an opportunity to talk to another fifteen-year-old girl, so I said I'd meet her at the front gate after last period.

As we walked home together with the Miami sun on the backs of our necks, Rachel and I talked about music we listened to and television shows we liked, and she never asked about my family or moving or if I had cried when I tried to call her. We started walking home together every day of the week, and then, she came over to meet Dad and Val. I quickly learned that she was well-known around school because she and her Free Hugs sign had been covered in the school paper the year before. She was a big fan of the *Twilight* book series, and although I had never read any of them, I looked them up online so I could pretend to like them so she would keep hanging out with me after school.

Team Edward! we said when we talked about our favorite characters in the books. We watched movies at her place in the afternoons and went swimming on the weekends. The phone call misunderstanding had become a sort of inside joke between us.

We had been spending time together for a few weeks when I decided to tell her about the murder. I had managed to pull off a few nightmare-free sleepovers with her, and we'd started a tradition of making scrambled eggs and bacon when we woke up in the mornings, so I thought there was nothing that could make her back out of our friendship now. Besides, I just wanted to *tell* someone. Get it out into the world. Stop carrying it around every day. We walked to one of our usual places, a playground around the corner from our houses, and we sat on the swings sharing a can of pineapple soda. We liked to go there when the sun was setting, take off our shoes, and kick up the sand with our bare feet as we pushed each other back and forth on the swings.

I want to tell you something about me, I said. *But I've never told anyone before.* She looked down at the sand beneath us, gripping the rusted chains of her swing between her hands. I told her everything: how loud the screams were and how dark the house was and how I had no idea what was going on. I didn't know yet how to sum it up, to make it concise and painless for the person listening.

You know what, you don't have to, like, walk me through it, she interrupted, looking down as she spoke. I stopped talking, realizing how stupid it was to tell Rachel about this here, or anywhere.

I'm so sorry, I said, and I started shaking.

You know why that happened to your grandma right? she asked. I shook my head, shocked that she might have the answer I had been looking for all summer. *Because you don't believe. Your mother is a sinner, and you and your brother have denied the power of Jesus Christ for too long.*

I didn't know what to say. I'd never wanted so badly for someone to have just told me that everything happens for a reason or what doesn't kill us makes us stronger.

I have to go, I said, and then, I picked up my shoes and ran home barefoot. When I got there, sticky from sweat and tears, I tried to catch my breath before I told Dad and Val I wouldn't be hanging out with Rachel anymore.

I went back to walking home alone, and a few days later, Ms. Graham asked me to stay after class.

How are you doing, really? she asked, like everyone did. But this time, it felt like she meant it. I told her all about Rachel, blurting out the whole story at once.

She told me I could come by her classroom during lunch period if I wanted, so I did. I started packing my lunch and eating it in one of the wooden desks across from her every afternoon. One day, as she ate her salad and I ate my sandwich, I finally brought up the story she'd told the class about the murders on her family's farm. She told me I was the first person she'd ever met who talked to her about it like it wasn't something from a crime drama on TV.

They turned it into a movie, you know? The worst thing that ever happened in my family is entertainment. People don't understand that it's reality.

I thought for a long time about that, wondering if I would have preferred if Rachel had wanted me to entertain and shock her. How much time would pass before I would be ready to tell someone else? Would anyone ever know what to say? I told Ms. Graham that the person who killed her family members was executed on the same day my grandma had been killed five years later. She looked at me with tears in her eyes.

That's a terrible day, now, isn't it?

I couldn't see the driver behind the wheel of the small white car following me after school, their face hidden behind the glare of the sun on the windshield. The car was never directly behind mine, never close enough for me to see who was inside. Immediately, I imagined it was Mom. A year had passed, but some days, the only thing I remembered was the way she looked with her bloodstained socks on the gravel driveway, running into the black night howling. In bed when I dreamt, I saw her running almost every night—only, in my dreams, it was always Mom chasing *me* as Betty died.

I knew it was impossible for Mom to be the driver of the white car on some random afternoon, but I knew that she was still angry with me, too. For a year, she'd written me letters asking, *Why did you tell them there's something wrong with me? I'm your mother.* She wrote, *Why did you tell them I'm a murderer?* She still asked me why I told the police she had a gun in the house, why Nick told them she was never a real parent to us.

He said it was like growing up with another child in the house, she said angrily into the phone in a line of other women waiting to call their family members. *What the fuck is wrong with you guys? I'm your mother!* But still, I answered each time she called, no matter what I was doing. I walked out of movie theaters, pulled over on the side of the highway, cupped my hand over the speaker at the beach. She asked me to go online and look up how to dye your hair with coffee grounds or Kool-Aid powder.

You wouldn't believe my roots, she said. I wrote down the instructions, mailed them to her inside a floral greeting card. I responded to her letters, printed out song lyrics to send to her, tried to tell her what was going on in my life. When I was home alone after school, I checked each room to make sure she wasn't there, waiting for me in her stained sweatpants. Nick didn't talk to her much anymore, so I was the one who heard it all: the anger, the despair, the fixation on finding someone else to blame. She'd blamed the murder on her ex-boyfriend, but he wore an ankle monitor with a GPS tracker on it. Then she blamed it on his cousins from the neighborhood. Then she blamed it on one of his exes. I was torn between being terrified of her and wanting her to love me.

When I'd get off the phone with her, I'd cry to music about romantic love and breakups, Taylor Swift's songs about loving a boy who would never love her back. That kind of music was the only thing that captured the heartache I felt. It was hyperbolic and exaggerated, but nothing else felt true. In my mind, Mom had become a villain from a horror movie, a shadow hiding between the clothes hanging in my closet, waiting for me behind the shower curtain. So I kept my eyes on my rearview mirror, sweat sticking between my palms and the steering wheel.

When I turned into our neighborhood, the white car finally disappeared. I never watched crime shows anymore, but the scene reminded me of them: an anxiety-inducing car chase, even if it was just inside my head.

It's not her, I said to myself, the way my therapist did when I told her about my nightmares, and how it felt like Mom was always in the office with me, hearing me say that I was afraid of her.

Your mother is locked up on the other side of the country. Your mother can't hurt you. But sometimes, secretly, I felt guilty for thinking prison was the solution to all of this. Where Mom was didn't change the fact that any of it had happened. And maybe, I told myself, she didn't deserve to be there in the first place.

I breathed a sigh of relief when I lost sight of the car, quickly parked in the driveway, and ran inside the house.

Calm down, I told myself in the mirror. *Nothing bad is happening.* It was a Friday; I was going to drop my backpack off at home and see a movie with a friend that afternoon. Nobody was home from work yet. My curfew was earlier than every other sixteen-year-old I knew because Dad and Val knew what kinds of things I saw some nights when it got too late. As soon as I pulled out of the driveway to leave again, the white car appeared again, parking right behind me and blocking me into the driveway.

I panicked again, my fingers slick with sweat as I reached to lock the doors. A man in a polo shirt got out and approached my car slowly, banging his knuckles on the window, saying my full name over and over again. Asking me who I was. Asking me to confirm my identity. I knew he wasn't a police officer, but the way he said my name reminded me of that day at the station. It reminded me of the way my face looked in the mirror of the interrogation room when the detectives asked me if Mom had a history of violence. In the car, I was crying now while he watched me, repeating my name. I didn't know what to do. I didn't know what he wanted or why he had been following me, but I was scared that he knew Mom, that something bad was going to happen again.

Yes, I mouthed through the window. *It's me. Please leave me alone. Please go away.*

These are for you, he said, holding up a packet of paperwork. I remembered how, several months earlier, after Mom got an attorney to represent her in the trial, Dad told Nick and me that we might be ordered to testify.

When I finally rolled down my window, my hand trembling with sweat, I wished that Nick had been in the car with me. To hold my hand, to talk to the man outside the door, explain the situation to him.

Wait, I'm a minor, I said, wiping my forehead. *I'm only sixteen. No one else is home right now.* I thought that I had won, that he was going to have to get back in his car and leave after he'd waited for me outside of the school parking lot and trailed behind me so closely. But he didn't get in his car and leave. Instead, he said he'd wait until my parents got home to receive the paperwork. I texted my friend, told her I'd gotten sick.

No movie for me, I said. *Sorry. :(*

The trial lasted five days during the summer before my senior year. I had been living with Dad and Val for over a year by then, trying to settle into some version of a normal teenaged life. We all ate dinner together at a dining table every night, asked how each other's day went. If not for the murder lingering in the background of it all, someone might think we looked like a normal family. The first two days of testimony were mostly cops and experts, the detectives who questioned us at the house, in the driveway, at the police station. They mostly talked about the blood. Mostly, the *spatter*. How the type of spatter depends on how fast the blood leaves the blood source or what amount of force is applied to the blood source.

There were passive stains, transfer stains, impact stains.

There was impact spatter, which happens when a blood source receives a blow or force that causes random, smaller drops of blood to disperse.

There were cast-off stains, which happen when blood is projected or flung in motion or when motion suddenly stops. They happen when a bloodstained object moves back and forth, *swings*, before applying force again.

There's fucking blood everywhere, Nick had said into the phone.

I get stuck on this phrase: *blood source*. Isn't it just a part of a body? Isn't it just a human being, their body, their flesh? Isn't it a person? In this case, wasn't it Betty?

When they played the 9-1-1 call over the speaker in the courtroom, Mom's lawyer approached the bench, told the judge, *She's having a hard time with this.*

Was it because of how my voice sounded over the speaker, so shaky and young? Was it because of her own wailing in the background? Was it because it brought her back to that night? I wondered how many nights she had spent back there, trapped in that same moment I couldn't escape. I wondered what her triggers were, what her flashbacks looked like. Did she ever hear Betty's screams howling through her cell? We wrote letters and spoke on the phone but never about this. She had wanted to testify, but her attorney advised against it. Maybe he knew she might lose it, might not be able to control herself.

We're going to take a short, five-minute recess, the judge said. When everyone returned to the courtroom moments later, they resumed playing the call as if nothing ever happened.

On the second day, she stood up and ran from the defense table while they played a VHS tape of one of her interviews with the detective.

Take a short five-minute recess so the defendant can compose herself, the judge said to the jury. In the video, Mom tells the detective the reasons why she couldn't have killed Betty, wouldn't have.

She's my sole support.

She pays my bad checks.

She supports my children.

Then: *I mean, right now, if I'm not going to prison or the electric chair, I'm going to a homeless shelter.*

Before the witness from the coroner's office, the forensic pathologist, was sworn in to testify, Mom asked her lawyer if she could be excused.

You have the right to be here, and you understand that, said the judge.

Yes, said Mom in her suit.

After she left, the witness described the autopsy he performed on Betty, the types of wounds he found on and inside of her. He talked about skin, how it *flexes* when stabbed. When asked about the weapon he thought might have caused the wounds, he said, *The knife they brought to the autopsy was a typical kind of steak knife that you might see in your kitchen. And all the wounds that we saw in the body were consistent with having been inflicted by a knife similar to that.*

It wasn't *the* knife, but maybe, it was part of the same set from our kitchen drawer.

He talked about the wounds. The seven stab wounds to her neck and chest, one of them having hit a major blood vessel, the subclavian artery, and another having pierced her upper lung. Two wounds on the back of her neck that had entered her skull, puncturing her spinal cord. Seven wounds on her back. Defensive wounds on her hands.

Betty was a fighter, the prosecutor told the jury.

The day before I was scheduled to testify, the prosecutor approached the judge as the court prepared for the last witness of the day.

One issue, Judge, with the daughter, is A.D. was very emotional today, she said. *I want to be sure there's no such emotion when her daughter comes in to testify. She's already fragile. She's scared to death to confront her mother, Judge.*

The judge replied, *I've instructed [the defense attorney] to instruct his client that she is not to run out of the courtroom. If she does that, we're going to have to shackle her to the little ring underneath the thing to make sure she doesn't leave. . . . I can't order someone not to cry.*

From where I sat on the stand, Mom looked so different at the defense table. She had become unrecognizable because she had become so *plain.* I was only used to seeing her beautiful and glamorous, full makeup on almost all the time, even for trips to pick up fast food or make a deposit at the bank.

You never know who you might meet, she used to say as she dusted her nose with powder or glossed her lips in the rearview mirror of the car. She used to always remind me of the importance of blinking slowly while applying mascara and using a sponge to blend liquid foundation in smooth circles across my skin. But there were no hair dyes or nail polishes or compacts filled with pressed powder here. This was the first time she couldn't be anybody but herself.

I was older now, had cut all my hair off and gotten my driver's license. Dad sat toward the back of the courtroom beside Dr. Finch, my old school-appointed psychiatrist who used to see me every week. They both had tears in their eyes. I wore a striped Hollister button-down shirt and glasses rather than my contacts so I would look smart, trustworthy, believable. Someone who knew what they were talking about. Years later, I'd look back and ask myself, why did I have to wear *flip-flops*? The Old Navy kind from the endless wall of dollar sandals, every color. Never mind that the night before I'd vomited Haagen Daz ice cream all over my favorite Vans, so they were propped up in the hotel bathtub to dry. Flip-flops: what a stupid shoe to wear to anything important, let alone your mother's murder trial.

When I saw Mom, I couldn't take my eyes off her. She didn't look at me, not once. I guessed I thought she would. That she might like my new hair, might think my makeup looked good. That I might have done something right. She was like a stranger to me, a woman who'd spent over a year living in a jail cell. Someone who looked almost nothing like the mother I knew. I couldn't stop staring at her hair. It was limp and longer than I'd ever seen it, gray roots sneaking out from the crown of her head.

I didn't know what you were supposed to wear to a murder trial. Something professional and conservative, something that made you look good but not too good. After all, a murder trial is different for a woman sitting at the defense table than a man. I had never seen Mom wear a suit before, and this one was a little too big for her, draped over her narrow shoulders like a hand-me-down or a last-minute Halloween costume.

It reminded me of how once, in elementary school, Nick had to dress up as one of the Founding Fathers for a school project with a group of other boys. He needed a suit, something grown-up, and Mom pulled this big, purple blazer out of her closet and handed it to him. On her bedroom dresser was the cemetery of orange pill bottles she relied on each day.

I need a tranquilizer, she'd said. Then she'd pop a Klonopin into her mouth, sometimes swallowing it dry without even a glass of water. Then her voice would change, and she'd start acting almost like a child, her mannerisms and speech pattern exaggerated, but she didn't seem to notice.

I need to lie down, she'd say.

When Nick wore the blazer to school, alongside the other kids wearing little-boy-sized black blazers, he looked out of place, nothing like a Founding Father. I didn't know where the jacket had even come from, or what Mom had worn it for in the past. Even as a kid, I wondered what other sides there were to Mom—what other selves she might have hidden all those years.

When I was little, I used to love wearing Mom's clothes when she wasn't home, and sometimes, I'd sit in front of the mirror with her eyeliners and lipsticks and blush to make my face look more like hers. When she had dates or parties to go to, I loved watching her get dressed to go out, the way she'd swipe golds, browns, and greens across her eyelids and blend the colors together with her fingertips.

Men always notice our eyes, she'd say proudly, blinking again and again to coat her eyelashes in black mascara like a spider's legs. I loved that she said *our* because it meant we were the same. Now, I didn't know what it would mean if I looked like Mom, acted like Mom, wore the same clothes as Mom. When I saw her in the courtroom, I wondered, what would I look like if I were going on trial for murder?

I've evaluated over a thousand females in criminal legal situations. People feel stripped of everything in jail. You don't have clothing, you don't have makeup, you don't have jewelry, and as a female, those things are important to most women.

Of all those women I've seen, not one other than A.D. has said I just feel awful because I don't have make up. . . .

I mean, for her she can't stand the thought of having any gray hairs. So she's been so desperate about this that she's been trying to dye her hair with coffee out at the detention center. It is rather unbelievable the extent to which she goes with this.

—Forensic Neuropsychologist's Testimony, *State v. A.D.*, 2009

The victim advocate they assigned to me had agreed to stay with me all day, even when I went on the stand during the testimony.

You'll really sit with me? I asked shakily. I'd felt like that all day, though the tears hadn't come yet. Like the night of the murder, how I managed not to cry at the house or in the police car, not even once. Ever since then, though, I cried almost all the time. At school, in the car, in the shower. Sometimes, I just couldn't control it.

You'll sit with me in front of everyone? I asked again, to be sure. I didn't understand that this was just her job, not some selfless gesture from the kindness of her heart. The judge let her bring a plastic trash can up to the stand with us in case I got sick again like the night before.

When you're in there, the jury staring at you, reporters writing down the things you're saying, you can't help but compare it to what you've seen on TV. I thought of *Law & Order*, the reruns we'd watched on the DVR night after night, right next to the room where Betty was killed.

All they wanted to know about were the sounds and the time and why I didn't get out of bed earlier.

Q: What was it that woke you up?

A: Screaming.

Q: Do you know what time this was?

A: 1:58.

Q: How do you know what time it was?

A: 'Cause I looked at my phone.

Q: In fact, was it 1:58 or—

A: 1:58.

Q: But close enough to 2:00?

A: Yeah.

Q: What did you think when you checked the time on your phone?

A: I thought the noise was the TV, because who would be screaming at 2:00 in the morning, so I don't know.

Q: Whose TV did you think it was?

A: My brother's.

Q: Did you come to—was it, in fact, his TV?

A: No.

Q: Do you know what happened or who was screaming?

A: Yeah.

Q: What happened? Can you tell the jury?

A: I heard screaming, saying, "Help me, I'm burning." And then I was like, scared, and I didn't want to go out of my room, and I thought that Betty was just having a bad dream or something, because she sometimes talked in her sleep, and so I didn't leave my room for a few minutes.

Q: Why didn't you leave your room right away?

After more questions about the blood on Mom's shirt, how it looked like barbecue sauce according to my deposition from earlier that week, the attorney asked me to repeat everything that had happened again.

Q: Unfortunately, Kristi, I want to go back to what you heard when you first woke up. Can you—you went through it pretty quickly. Can you think about it and recall the sequence of what you heard and then tell the jury where you were when you heard those words and who you think said them?

Next, the attorney asked me to talk about how Mom reacted after the murder first happened, back when I didn't even realize that a murder had happened.

Q: How do you know she was upset?

A: Because she was like, crying and screaming and breathing a lot.

Q: What do you mean by breathing a lot?

A: I don't know, she was hyperventilating.

Q: Do you think she was having a panic attack?

A: Yeah.

Q: And had you seen her—how many times beforehand had you seen her having a panic attack?

A: I've only seen her have one real one. The other ones were like small ones.

Q: How do you know that they were panic attacks?

A: Well, because one time in fifth grade we went to Walmart to buy school supplies, and it was really, really, expensive, and it was a lot of stuff, and I don't know, she just was like, this is so much money, and she started freaking out and breathing really loud and crying in Walmart, and I figured it was a panic attack.

I wasn't there when the guilty verdict was announced. Dad and I were on the plane back to Florida already. I was supposed to take the SAT the following week, start thinking about college. The newspapers said the *jury took a little more than an hour* to convict her.

I've never seen a jury in a murder trial come back so fast, Mom's attorney told a reporter for the *Santa Fe New Mexican.*

Over a year had passed and still, none of the people around me would say the word *murder* or even speak Betty's name unless I did it first. Nick, especially, tried to pretend that nothing had ever happened. He had cried once after we scattered Betty's ashes and then never again—at least not in front of me. I had never seen him cry before the day we stood on top of the hill where we said goodbye to Betty, but he came close one afternoon in elementary school when he fell off his skateboard and scraped his elbow. He just kept lying there on the street next to a mailbox, blood dripping down the back of his arm as he told me not to tell anyone about this.

That was before we really knew Betty, or even Craig, when we still lived in a warm house in the North Carolina mountains where we raced each other on skateboards, roller blades, and bikes. Before we moved around from town to town and state to state. Before Betty took us in, gave us a home. It made me sad to think about that when I watched him cry so hard he sank to his knees beside the empty bag where Betty's ashes used to be. I thought of how far away we were from that curve in the street where his skin broke against the black asphalt, how he looked even smaller when we lost Betty eight years later.

Nick dropped out of college after the first semester. Packed up his dorm, said goodbye to the baseball players he shared it with. He wasn't interested in his classes, couldn't focus on the work. He never said why, what exactly was holding him back. Maybe none of us ever asked. There were days when I wanted to sit down and say, *Tell me why you've only cried about Betty once,* but I knew how selfish and childish it would be. Sometimes I thought about just walking up to him and saying, *Tell me everything you remember about the night she died,* but I was too afraid. It couldn't have been just me being consumed by the memories. I wanted to give him space, let him deal with it in the ways that made sense to him—even if that meant not dealing with it at all. But I was afraid, too, that his silence made our experience invisible. If I couldn't talk about that night with the one person who might understand how I was feeling, had it even happened at all?

Everyone else—Dad and Val and my school counselor, Mr. Henry—tiptoed around me, afraid that calling these things what they were might make me *do* something. In the beginning, I had talked about wanting to die. I had cried in the hotel room on the nights following the murder and asked out loud, *What's the point of living if it hurts all the time?* I didn't know that hurt would last so long. I had spent the summer waking up every night at the same time that I had heard Betty screaming, and I sometimes wondered if dying was the only way to make it stop. Maybe everyone around me thought that avoiding saying Betty's name would make the way she died hurt less or make my memories of her death disappear. But it felt like my memories of her life were starting to disappear, too.

I was grateful that Dad and Val and Mr. Henry were worried about me, but I wanted them to be honest with me. Dr. Elliot kept prescribing me sleeping medication and antidepressants, and Dad and Val kept saying, *You don't need those.* I never took the pills, but I never asked Dad or Val what they thought I needed instead. They thought that I was still too fragile right now, but that things would get better over time.

You don't want to get hooked on those things like—Dad would say when we talked about the medication. His face would turn red, and he'd look embarrassed while he finished saying it: *You know, like your mom.*

Dad and Val's fears about the medication made sense, but the truth was I couldn't sleep. It was hard getting through some days so tired, so confused and sad. I didn't know how to keep my grief from spilling out into every part of my life, so I did what I thought I was supposed to do: I tried to hide it, to shrink it, to make it go away. I stopped telling them about my nightmares, about my fears, about women I saw in the school halls or the grocery store parking lot who looked a lot like Mom. I started to think my own grief was toxic and ugly and uncomfortable, that it would stain everything and everyone it touched.

When I was alone, I picked at my skin, the hair on my arms and eyebrows. The pain felt kind of good, almost normal. There was nothing I could do but keep it all to myself. Conversations with other people about the murder felt awkward and uncomfortable, starting and ending with clichéd lines that never seemed to fit. I knew it was easier for people to email me quotes from *When Bad Things Happen to Good People* and say things like, *Everything happens for a reason* or *She's in a better place now.* Each time, I had to stop myself from asking if they thought Mom was in a better place now, too.

Vanessa's mom had killed herself that summer before senior year, while I was away at Mom's trial. The whole school had heard about it on the news after she called 9-1-1 and cried into the speaker when she found her mother. I didn't really know Vanessa well, but she sat in the row of desks beside me in first period Environmental Science class every morning. Now, she sat across from me in a circle of six people clenching tissues and old family photographs in their trembling fists. This was the first meeting of the grief group started by our guidance counselor.

After I returned to school in the fall of my senior year, Mr. Henry had called me into his office.

How did it go? he asked. He was referring to the trial. He wasn't a stranger to my *situation,* as he and my other teachers called it, because Dad and Dr. Elliot had contacted him when I moved to the school. Since then, he called me into his office regularly to ask questions like, *How are you feeling today?* and *Is everything okay at home?*

I'm so tired of being like this, I said when he asked me about the trial.

Like what?

Different. Like I'll never be my old self again.

He said he wanted to tell me about the new group he started.

Grief Group! he said enthusiastically. *Everyone I've invited to come to the group is just like you. They're all just as sad, scared, and confused as you are.* I didn't tell Dad or Val exactly what the group was about. Instead, I called it an after-school club or a study group—a place where I might even make some friends.

The group met for the first time after school in Mr. Henry's cramped office.

This is a safe space for talking and listening about the loss of our loved ones, he began. *Some of you may know each other, and some of you may be strangers.*

There were six of us: five girls and one boy. Were we really the only six people in our whole high school who had lost someone? Maybe we were just the only ones whose parents or therapists had asked Mr. Henry to keep an eye on them.

Who would like to begin? he asked.

I came home one day and there she was, Vanessa said. *Dead.* Her voice cracked a little when she talked about her mother's suicide. Her hair was the color of a penny, full of tightly wound curls that were frizzy at the ends. I couldn't help but wonder if her mother's hair had looked like that, too. She told us about the blood on the walls of the bathroom, how it still didn't seem real that her mom was gone. She said, *You never think something this bad will happen to you.* I wanted to ask Vanessa if she was mad at her mother for dying on purpose and leaving without saying goodbye, but she only told us how much she missed her.

I thought about the Vanessa who came to class and sat three feet away from me five days a week to take notes in a blue binder. We weren't friends, but we talked every morning: I always asked her how she did on last week's quiz or where she was thinking about applying to college. I'd never asked her if she knew that daughters weren't supposed to watch their mothers bleed. The worst part about the grief group was that I couldn't stop picturing the bodies.

I'd never seen Josh around school before, but I listened closely as he told the group about his sister's accident. He was tall, wearing a black hooded sweatshirt and jeans that rose above his ankles when he sat down. He told us about the day his sister and her boyfriend took the family's jet ski out to a narrow canal near their neighborhood in North Miami.

They didn't want to drive out to the ocean, he said. He told us he had a bad feeling that day, that he started running toward the canal to find them. He wanted to tell them to stop, to turn around, to please come back home. He was silent for a moment, and then, his voice cracked like Vanessa's.

It was too late, he said. By the time he caught up with them, they had crashed into the wall of the canal, and his sister was killed instantly. She was decapitated when she was ejected from the back of the jet ski. He trembled as he told us what it was like to see parts of her skull on the ground beneath him.

Her brain, he began, but he couldn't finish the sentence. I was having a hard time listening now. I could only think of the canal near my own house, how the narrow stream of water running through it was so dirty that it matched the concrete walls on either side.

Vanessa's right, he said. *You never think anything this bad could ever happen. And then it does.*

Josh forgot to bring a photograph of his sister, or maybe, it was too painful to flip through the pages of his mom's old photo albums. I would never know what his sister looked like in those photos—when she was alive—but I hated how I couldn't stop imagining how she looked after. I pictured her boyfriend standing helpless in the shallow water, wearing a bloodstained T-shirt but no lifejacket. I could almost see her blood pooling at the surface of the gray water, inching toward him as he cried with his head in his hands while Josh stood at the edge of the canal and watched.

Kate told us about the cancer in her father's lungs, how she felt his hand turn cold as he finally slipped away in a white hospital bed. It was harder for me to picture this one: maybe Kate sat in a vinyl chair at the edge of his bed and held his hand until even the tube inside him couldn't help him breathe. I didn't have much experience with hospitals, and I wondered if Vanessa and Josh were trying to see Kate's dad, too. I didn't want to be the only one comparing my pain to everyone else's. What was it like to hold someone while they died? What did it feel like to *touch* death, not just listen to it from a bedroom down the hall?

It was a comfort to know that people in my classes had actually been there when someone they loved had stopped living, whether they felt it or heard it or walked in after it happened. Listening to everyone else pour their grief out into the circle, I started to feel safe there, like I was allowed to show them all the places where it still hurt. At the beginning of the meeting, Mr. Henry said, *Remember: it's okay to be broken. That's why we're all here.*

I wanted to sound how the others did when they talked about their loved ones. I wanted my voice to crack in the right place when I told Josh and Vanessa that it was too late by the time I found my loved one, too. But I already knew what they were going to think: everyone has to experience the death of a grandparent in their lives. It wasn't nearly as bad as losing a parent or sibling. So I'd have to tell them that Betty didn't *just* die.

She was murdered, I would say, and then, they would understand.

I wondered if the group would be offended if I talked about losing Mom. Maybe they'd be right if they were offended because she didn't die. I knew it wasn't the same, but I hoped I would be allowed to tell the group that sometimes it felt like Mom did die. Just two months earlier, she'd been convicted of second-degree murder. Her sentencing was coming up in a month, two days after I would turn seventeen. I didn't know how long she'd be gone, what could happen during that time. I didn't want the group to think I was insensitive or that I thought I knew what they were going through when I really didn't. But I knew it wasn't the same because my own mother was alive in a cell with dozens of other mothers and daughters who'd done something they couldn't take back.

Even as I heard the other stories, I still felt alone in my grief—not just because I had lost two people but because one of them was responsible for the loss of the other. I didn't want the group to blame me for Betty's death like Rachel had, so I decided not to tell them about her screams—how they had echoed across the house, each one longer and louder than the last—while I just lay there waiting. I didn't want them to know about the fear or the blood or the hours I spent locked in the back of the police car. I didn't want them to know that I was afraid of speaking in front of groups of people, how it reminded me of sitting in front of the judge and the jury again, hoping I could say the right thing to fix it, make it all go away.

When it was my turn to share my loss with the group, I couldn't look at anyone. I sat in my chair with my head down and picked at the polish on my fingernails. When I started to talk about Betty and Mom, I thought maybe the others would start to think that I wasn't any different from the rest of them.

I never thought anything this bad would happen to me either, I said, agreeing with Vanessa and Josh, letting them know I was grateful that I could finally admit that out loud. I began to tell them about the blood on my mother's hands, how it had dried on the inside of her fingers.

I told them how some days I still felt as scared as I did when I dialed 9-1-1 and held the phone up to my ear with my sweating palm. Vanessa had dialed 9-1-1, too, and I wanted to tell her that I knew how she felt. I couldn't remember the last time I had been so honest about the fear or how it still snuck up on me even over a year later, so I looked up. I wanted to see the group again and tell them I was relieved, that I felt safe here, but then I saw the looks on their faces: hands covering their mouths and tissues drying their tears as they all stared at me in disbelief.

I thought I could be as brave as the people who'd only let their voices crack and their hands shake while they talked about the loved ones who were missing from their lives now, but I couldn't stop the tears from rolling down my face. I was reliving it—the blood on the walls and on the sheets and on the insides of Mom's hands—right there in the guidance counselor's office. The worst part was looking up and seeing the whole grief group crying, too. They were shocked, scared, and sad just like me. I kept looking at Josh, Kate, and Vanessa, thinking, *Come on, I'm just like you.* Somehow, I felt more alone than I did when we all walked separately in those hallways and classrooms thinking that grief had never done to others what it had done to us. Didn't Vanessa ever think—the way her mom had, the way I still did—that maybe dying would be easier than living with so much pain?

Maybe I hoped that one of the stories in the circle would be the one to scare me, to make my face burn red as I put my hands over my own mouth in horror. I wanted Josh to be angry with his sister's boyfriend for taking her to the canal. I wanted Vanessa to be angry with her mother for leaving her behind to find the blood in the bathtub one day during summer vacation. I didn't want to be different. I didn't want to be the girl whose mother was a murderer, the girl whose story shocked and scared people who'd already suffered losses of their own.

I just wanted to be a member of the group, to have a place to go after school where I could finally tell the truth about my grief. But my kind of loss didn't belong there. I brought what I'd lost to the group and hoped to find people I could share it with, but I felt more alone than I did before I walked into the room. I watched the strands of Vanessa's copper hair stick to the tears on her face and wondered what would happen when I sat down next to her in science class, both of us knowing now that maybe grief couldn't be shared the way we thought it could.

PART THREE Searching

Near the end of my first semester of college, I decided to visit Mom. I booked the flight, got a hotel, arranged a ride from the airport to the prison with my old boyfriend from the ninth grade. The prison would only allow me to come at a certain time of the week, so I had to explain the circumstances to my professors and ask to take my finals early. They agreed, many of them with that same surprised, sad look I'd get any time I told anyone about the murder, about Mom. I wasn't a bad student, but I wasn't a great one either.

Are you sure you want to do this? asked one concerned professor. *Is it going to be safe for you to be alone with her?*

She didn't do anything, I explained. *Don't worry. She's not dangerous. Trust me: I was there when it happened.*

I hated that I had been there, that I had heard Betty dying down the hall, but I still couldn't say whether or not Mom had killed her. Mom had insisted she was innocent so many times that it was easier to agree with her and hope that I would eventually start to believe it. I'd tell her over the phone that I couldn't wait until she got out, that our lives were going to go back to normal someday, but even then, I knew I didn't mean it. I couldn't imagine what normal would look like after all of this—even if she had been proven innocent.

I had moved three hours north of Dad, Val, and Nick for college, started trying to create a life for myself, an identity. I was glad high school was over, and I hoped this would be a fresh start. Getting in had been hard, almost impossible. I applied to five schools and only got into one with the requirement that I attend the summer session to take introductory classes to catch up, get on track. I had taken the SAT three times before I even broke a score of one thousand. I felt stupid, worthless. I used to love reading, used to impress Betty with how smart I was. Since she died, I could barely focus in class and couldn't keep my dark thoughts away during long assignments or tests. I kept the worn copy of *The Outsiders* that she bought for me on one of our Saturday morning outings in my dorm, though I could never bring myself to read it again.

After the cross-country flight to New Mexico, I was nervous to see Mom. Over the phone, she told me prison was the worst place in the world, worse than anything I could ever imagine. I tried to be there for her, support her, even when all I wanted was for her to support me.

I stand in front of the vending machine pressing all the soda buttons, she said. *When it lights up, it's the closest thing to a slot machine I've seen in years.* Later, when I told a friend about this, he replied, *Those people are allowed to drink Coke?* Mom told me she felt sorry for all of the other women there—that nobody *out there* could ever understand. For the rest of their lives, she said, they'd be seen as worthless criminals and addicts.

I hadn't seen her since the trial, and I'd been trying to scrub the sight of her at the defense table from my mind ever since. After she was found guilty, the newspaper published Mom's face on the front page again. She stood with the black oversized blazer draped over her shoulders, holding her head in her hands with her attorney beside her. There had been so many articles about us, about Mom, over the years with provocative headlines like, *Kids Say Mom Was Covered in Blood* or *Stabber Gets Fifteen Years,* but that spread of her at the trial was one of the worst images I'd ever seen. Every time I thought of that photo, I feared I was going to vomit.

Since I was coming from another state, the prison staff arranged for us to have what would normally be called a conjugal visit—usually for married couples to be alone—in a small trailer with bedrooms and a full kitchen. I was allowed to bring groceries to cook a real meal for Mom, but we weren't allowed to use any sharp objects, so I had to be strategic that morning at Walmart when I bought the food. I decided on sandwiches, something that would be simple enough to make but would hopefully be much better than what Mom was used to eating.

I was on the verge of physical illness by the time I walked through the metal detector, hands shaking. Would she like the food I brought? What would she think of my hair? Had I painted my nails the right color? Would she be mad about the flavor of pie I picked out from the Walmart bakery? Did she even like pie? Would we have anything to talk about? The guards brought us to the trailer separately, one after the other, and then, they stood outside for the duration of our visit.

Seeing Mom felt like the lucid dreams I'd been having since I started college. I had a hard time sleeping alone in my dorm, so I'd reverted to sleeping with the lights on for months, then with an embarrassing children's nightlight I got at Target. I started taking NyQuil and melatonin together, hoping each night that I'd fall asleep quickly, before the bad thoughts could come to me as I stared at the ceiling of my room.

First, the combination had made me sick, but now, I was used to it. I would fall asleep, rest deeply, then wake up groggy, but at least I'd made it through the night. I had never touched alcohol—always hated it after those years watching Mom and Craig fight about it—but I assumed that must have been what a hangover felt like. The only problem was the lucid dreaming and then the sleep paralysis: sometimes I'd dream someone was breaking into my dorm, fully convinced they were in the room with me, but unable to move my body. Sometimes the intruder was Mom.

When I saw her in the trailer, I was stunned. Was this really her? She wore the prison-issued jumpsuit like the ones we both wore at the police station, had those pesky gray hairs snaking out at her roots. She had long hair now, down to her waist, stick straight from the dry desert climate. We sat on the couch and talked, and I kept reminding myself to act normal. She told me she didn't like my boots, reminded me how we always used to disagree about clothes. We'd fight at the mall or in the aisles at Ross, and she'd end up wearing the jeans out of my dresser drawers anyway.

I don't know where you got your taste, she said, laughing.

I looked at her hands. I wasn't used to seeing her nails without shiny polish on them. Had she used these hands to kill Betty, whether or not she was in her right mind? What stood out the most were her eyes. When I looked into them, I thought of the night of the murder. How she stood in the doorway, her eyes black and lifeless.

Why are you looking at me like that? she asked, and I gasped, jumped back in my seat a little. I looked back at the door of the trailer, wondered if the guards were listening in. Maybe I was afraid of her after all.

I was drunk with my legs dangling in the deep end of the pool when a guy named Jason or James or Jack said he wanted to get to know me.

Y'know, like, what do your parents do? he asked, pushing his glasses up from the tip of his shiny nose. My friend's roommate said she wanted to sneak into the pool at a nearby apartment complex with a small group of friends and a twelve pack.

I was new to drinking, holding a thirty-two-ounce bottle of malt liquor in a brown paper bag. I had never held one before, and I didn't even like the taste, but I thought maybe I looked like someone else when I was drinking it. By eleven thirty, the small group had become a pool party, and I was slurring my words with Jason's hand on my knee. It must have been midnight by the time I asked him if he wanted to hear a story about Mom and me.

I'm a psych major, he said. *Everyone's always talking about how they're turning into their mothers.*

It wasn't the first time I'd ever told anyone in college about the murder, but it was the first time I told anyone after I'd been drinking.

She got fifteen years, I told him. At the time, it was the maximum sentence for second-degree murder in the state of New Mexico.

Damn! Jason said. *That's just like TV, like some* Law & Order *shit.* He wanted to know if my hand was on the Bible *and everything* when I went up to testify. He wanted to know if I had to swear to tell the truth, the whole truth, nothing but the truth so help me God. I didn't know why, but I wouldn't stop talking about it. For some reason, I couldn't stop. I told Jason about the screams like I'd told the jury about the screams back in 2009, how at first, all I heard was *I'm burning.*

Burning? Jason asked, and all I could do was nod. Even five years later, the sounds still rippled through my mind every now and then, sometimes out of nowhere—*I'm burning, I'm burning, I'm burning*—as if to remind me how long I'd stayed in bed, how long I'd let her go on screaming, dying.

Jason just wanted to know about the *weapon.* The word came out of his mouth slowly, like it was the first time it ever really meant something when he said it. He wanted to know what kind of murder it was. A shooting? Or worse? Was the weapon a gun, a knife, something even stranger? Was it something I'd used before, anything I recognized from around the house?

I told him the truth: I didn't know, even now. Maybe it had been a knife, but they never found the thing because of how fast everything happened that night. I told him the cops had taken my compass and protractor off my desk and added it to the big list of sharp objects they'd found during the investigation. Even then, I still found myself wondering, can you really kill someone with a compass and protractor?

I wanted to tell Jason about my writing, how I'd become an English major so I could write. Read more, like I used to with Betty. How I thought that if I remembered everything, got it all down on the page, I could be free. I'd started doing well in school, taking creative writing and literature classes. Getting back to my old self, some version of me that Betty would recognize. Maybe, if I could finally tell the story right, I could find out why she was killed while the rest of us were not.

Jason wanted to know if I ever wished she hadn't been.

Hadn't been what? I asked. I pretended that maybe I didn't hear him, that I was so drunk I'd forgotten what we were even talking about. But I knew what he wanted to know—did I ever wish that she hadn't been the one to die. Did I ever wish it had been Nick or me or even Mom who had died that night? He wanted me to confess that I'd thought about this, to tell him that if I could, I might wish the lacerations and the bleeding out—the detective's words that still haunted me—on someone else, or maybe even on myself.

I mean, there's no question that she did it right? Like, case closed? That's it? he asked. I shrugged.

I had been asked so many versions of this question over the years that I felt numb to it, tired of having to give other people the answer they wanted.

You were there. You should know, they'd always say. But the case was not simple, cut-and-dried like those we'd all seen on TV or movies, no matter how much I wished it could be that easy.

There were things that didn't add up, didn't make sense. There were things that gnawed at me some nights as I tried to fall asleep, sent me into dark rabbit holes on the internet, trying to find out what happens when you kill someone, the way Mom, Betty, and I had done when we tried to fact-check one of our crime shows. These things made me question whether the police had done all they could do to find out the truth. One night, Mom called me while I was studying, cried into the phone in that same old childish voice.

It was your brother, she said. *I'm here because I was just trying to protect him. I couldn't let my son go to prison.* I was horrified. I hung up and ran to the toilet to puke. I feared the next time she would call that she would bring this up again. When she did things like that—got upset, said things she couldn't take back, threatened to kill herself—she wouldn't call me again for days or weeks. I'd lose sleep, sit in class worried about her, wondering if she was okay. The next time she called, she didn't even mention it. I never brought it up again.

The weird thing was, I told Jason, choking down another sip at the pool, *I never thought she'd kill anyone but herself.*

He was pretending to be concerned now, staring down at my nervous hands wrapped around the brown bag. I knew it didn't really matter to him either way. After tonight, he wouldn't ever wonder again whether or not the right person had been in prison for Betty's murder. He just wanted to talk to some girl at a party.

Maybe he was imagining the contents of the glass bottle swimming through my veins, like the half-naked sorority girls coming up for air at the surface of the pool. Mostly, I assumed, he wanted to walk me to the car and take me to his place, show me the coffee table where I could put down my purse. Maybe he was wondering if there was a weapon—a knife or even a nine-millimeter gun—hiding somewhere inside of it.

Or maybe he thought he'd get lucky, end up in bed with the girl whose life reminded him of things he'd only ever seen on TV or in the pages of his psychology textbooks. But he didn't. They never did. The thought of undressing in front of anyone made my body ache, like an old wound flaring up after you get hurt in the same place too many times. No matter how much of the murder I chose to share with Jason, or with anyone, I never mentioned anything about that part. About putting my clothes in the evidence bag. That was something I couldn't bear to say out loud.

A.D. didn't protect her children. . . . She's not on trial for that, though. She's not on trial for being a bad mother. She's on trial for killing her own mother.

—Prosecutor, *State v. A.D.*, 2009

As I grew older, sometimes talking to men about that night made me feel powerful, like I scared them, forced them into shutting up and listening. Other times, it made me feel used, like I was some kind of freak—they could tune in for the gory details, then go home and laugh about what a crazy story it was with their friends. I'd get home and take my melatonin and NyQuil, just wish the memories would wash away during the night. Most of the time, I just wanted to talk to someone, anyone, about the pain. How it was so heavy it felt like it was crushing me all the time. How sometimes I wondered what would happen if I just let it. What if one day, I did what Mom always said she'd do? Just woke up and said, *Today, I'm going to stop trying to live through this.*

It wasn't the grief that made me want to die. It was the things that came with it, the smaller, everyday cruelties that reminded me how bad it was, how violent all of it had been. A crying baby made me jump while I waited in line to return something at the mall. I covered my eyes at the sight of a pool of blood in a movie that I used to love when I was in middle school. I broke down crying when I smelled that thick scent of cigarettes on someone's shirt as they walked by. It was still hard to look at knives, to pick them up and use them to cut the food I ate every day.

Year after year, because I kept so much bottled up inside me, it was hard to keep track of the details from my own lived memories of that night and those I'd read about in the newspaper or in the transcripts from the trial, even things I saw on TV. It was harder, too, to separate the flashbacks from the nightmares because I experienced both so often. The reminders were everywhere, and it was impossible to shut them off. Sometimes it felt like I was asking for them, like I deserved them, like the night I got a phone call from a blocked number and answered, thinking maybe it was Mom calling from jail.

Hello?

Help me! Help me! Your mom is trying to murder me!

Then a roar of laughter and a click. Maybe I had hoped the person on the line would be one who'd want to talk, someone who'd want to listen.

Some days I woke up wishing nobody would ever find out about it, and other days, I wanted to scream it at the top of my lungs, tell every person I saw what had happened that night. How I couldn't get the screaming out of my ears, that haunting sound of burning. How I couldn't get out of bed in the morning because it had taken me so long to fall asleep the night before. How I'd close my eyes and see it all, even the parts I'd learned from the files and the internet. How after all this pain, this loss, there were still so many parts to this story out there that weren't mine. That never even belonged to me.

When Grant picked me up outside my apartment, he said he was *so fucking stoked* about the movie he was taking me to see.

Scream 4, he said. *You like scary movies, right?*

I knew Grant well enough through mutual friends, but we didn't know any personal details about each other. We'd never been alone together. He didn't know about the murder, how I could still hear the screaming, the howling, even now. The volume was a little lower, and I slept through the night more often, but the sound still echoed in my ears.

Once you wake up to that high-pitched screaming, the kind that the women—because it's almost always the women who die—do in the movies, you don't pay to watch someone fake it. Instead, you become afraid of dying, but you can't really tell anyone. Being in a dark room is never the same again. Locking a door is never the same again. Going to sleep is never the same again. Everything you used to do becomes something else: you wake up, you could die. You go to sleep, you could die. I'd always wondered if Nick thought that way, too, but I could never bring myself to ask.

What's your favorite scary movie? Grant asked in a raspy, unsettling voice. I recognized the quote from the movie commercial I'd seen so many times back in elementary school. I didn't tell him I'd never seen any of the previous *Scream* movies or that I didn't want to see this one. I did that a lot: pretended, performed, tried to be someone I wasn't.

I was in the third grade when boys my age started wearing Ghostface costumes for Halloween. I'd seen the masks everywhere—Sears, Kmart, even the drugstore where Mom picked up her prescriptions—since *Scream 3* had come out that year. When I saw all the boys wearing hooded cloaks with long white chins and warped black eyes, I wondered how many had seen any of the movies. How many parents had let their eight-year-old sons watch it, dress up like the masked killer to trick-or-treat in our small town in North Carolina?

I was too afraid to watch, but everyone recognized the voice who asked, *What's your favorite scary movie?* The commercials gave me what I tried to describe to my friend at school as *bad thoughts*.

We all knew how it started: Drew Barrymore, popping popcorn with her blonde bob and her off-white sweater, answering the cordless phone we all had in our living rooms. Those of us who could only stomach the preview never knew that Drew Barrymore wasn't the star, that she didn't even survive the first few minutes of the film. Every time I'd see the commercial, I'd run into every room in the house. I'd flip every light switch, tiptoe into the bathroom to pull back the patterned plastic shower curtain, make sure nobody was hiding behind it.

There were the kids whose older siblings had left the VHS lying around, who'd later lie about having watched the whole thing without flinching. But really, they'd just read the cover front to back while no one was looking, then put a newspaper or magazine on top of it so they wouldn't have to see that face again. The blue-eyed girl with the hand over her mouth, waiting to die just like her friends. And there were those of us whose parents would watch the Blockbuster rental with the volume just high enough after our bedtime had come and gone, thinking we'd fallen fast asleep. Most of us would still be awake, secretly listening to the sound that gave the movie its title, hiding under our blankets and fearing the next time the phone would ring.

There was a moment when it seemed like everyone had forgotten about *Scream* and started talking about *The Matrix* instead. Kids would run around the playground asking, *Blue pill or red pill,* bending their bodies back like Neo while we played limbo at recess. But once *Scream* 3 came out, Ghostface was back. Once Halloween came around, I'd see a dozen boys in white masks and black robes, bending their elbows, pulling their clenched fists into the air, ready to strike their next victim.

I'd never seen Ghostface kill anyone, never found out who was really hiding beneath his mask, but still, I was terrified. I had nightmares about his face and his voice and would startle awake some nights in a cold sweat, fearing he was somewhere in the room with me. I was only four years old when the first one came out, and somehow, it felt like Ghostface—his mask, his voice, and especially his knife—had always been there, lurking in the background. I was not four anymore. In the car with Grant, I imagined what it might be like to tell him about Betty. To explain why I didn't watch slasher movies, why I wasn't a fan of blood and gore.

How cute, he said, when I told him I was nervous. He kept on driving. We got our tickets and sat down in silence. I wondered if anyone in the crowd could tell how scared I already was, how I began digging my nails into my skin.

After the first phone call, the movie begins with two false starts: sequential opening scenes from the films within the film, *Stab 6* and *7*, to trick the viewer. To blur the line between fantasy and reality. First, two teen girls—one I'd recognized as Darcy from the teen drama *Degrassi*—sit in the kitchen talking about a guy who'd been stalking one of them on Facebook. After Ghostface attacks them, the screen zooms out to show the title card for *Stab 6,* which two other teen girls are watching on the couch. The audience, including Grant, laughed at the graphic deaths of the teen girls as they were attacked by the man in the mask. I reached my hand inside my shirt sleeve, started digging my nails into the skin until it broke.

The blonde on the left, unimpressed by the film, asks, *A bunch of articulate teenagers sit around and deconstruct horror movies until Ghostface kills them one by one? It's been done to death. . . . Stick a fork in 1996 already.*

Soon, her friend pulls out a knife and stabs her, telling her to *shut the fuck up and watch the movie.* While everyone around me was entertained by the effects and the gratuitous fake blood, I stood up and ran out of the theater as the title card for *Stab 7* flashed across the screen. I couldn't breathe, flooded with thoughts of the knife that had never been found and the screams—the real kind—I'd heard that night.

Alone in the bathroom stall, a drop of blood soaking through my shirt sleeve, I wondered if Grant even noticed I'd left.

That night, after a friend picked me up from the theater, I lay in bed unable to sleep, haunted by my bad thoughts again: the flashbacks of Betty's death, the blood on the wall beside her bed, the hidden, lost-forever knife, the terror I felt then and still felt every time I had to relive it. After I turned the light on in my room, I ran out to my apartment's shared bathroom, pulled back the shower curtain. I wondered if Grant had been one of those boys who dressed up like Ghostface to scare girls in the school hallway just because he could.

I wanted to find out more about the movies that had lived in the darkest corners of my imagination for so long, even before Betty died. In a 1998 CNN interview, screenwriter Kevin Williamson told a story: he was scared to death when he wrote the opening scene of *Scream*. It was credited with reviving the slasher genre but was comical and over the top enough that it seemed to spoof itself.

I was watching this Barbara Walters special on the Gainesville murders, he recalled. He told the reporters how the crimes of the Gainesville Ripper—a series of 1990 stabbings that had shaken the small college town in north-central Florida—had scared him so bad he'd imagined an intruder had broken in through the window and left it open.

He didn't mention the details of the Gainesville killings, which included stalking, rape, and even decapitation in the case of the victim whose head had been posed on her dresser for her parents to find. After waking up from a nightmare in the middle of the night, thanks to that Barbara Walters special, Williamson explained, he got up and started writing about a masked killer who stalked a small town with a knife in his gloved hand.

A year earlier, Janet Frake gave an interview to a local Florida newspaper, the *Sarasota Herald-Tribune,* seven years after the Gainesville murders. Frake was the only victim who'd survived an attack by the Gainesville Ripper—before he'd become a media sensation complete with a nickname fit for prime-time TV. She explained how, just three days before the first attack in Gainesville, she'd returned to her Sarasota home with a rented video and a six pack of beer when a man in a black ski mask who'd been hiding in her bathroom attacked her, raping her at knifepoint.

Somehow, Frake explained, she'd convinced him not to go through with the rest, by inviting him to sit down for a beer. He offered to take off his mask, but she didn't want to see. She didn't want to have to remember his face. In the interview, Frake said, *To be honest, I thought it was a joke at first. Then you see a black mask and you see a knife.* The opening scene of *Scream,* which leaves Drew Barrymore's body bloodied and hanging from a tree for her parents to find when they get home, seems to say the same thing: all of this is just a joke.

The special Williamson had watched was an episode of ABC's news series, *Turning Point,* titled "Gainesville: The Price of Murder."

But who remembers the victims? Barbara Walters had asked in her opening remarks. It was 1994. Three years had passed since the Ripper, Danny Rolling, in a black hood, black mask, and black leather gloves, had attacked five University of Florida students.

The special detailed the tragic deaths of the five young people who were stabbed to death by Rolling over the course of three days in August 1990. In her bright red blazer, Walters sat viewers down in their living rooms and promised to do things differently than most *murder stories,* as she called them. She would highlight, maybe for the first time, the lives of the victims rather than the crimes of the perpetrator.

Starring news personalities Diane Sawyer and Peter Jennings, *Turning Point* was in its first season. The Gainesville special was the third episode, airing just two weeks after its premiere, "The Manson Women: Inside the Murders," showed Sawyer interviewing Charles Manson in prison. The '90s were rife with televised crime stories, with *Unsolved Mysteries* airing inside millions of our households and *Law & Order* already in its fourth season of telling the same story over and over.

Turning Point premiered three months before Nicole Brown Simpson and Ron Goldman were stabbed to death in Brentwood, California, and two years before the mysterious death of six-year-old JonBenét Ramsey. We invited Barbara Walters into our homes to show us the worst of humanity, and she convinced us never to look away. We didn't yet know these investigations—and others like them—would become an

American obsession that would endure for decades. We didn't yet know how long our eyes would be glued to the white Bronco speeding down a Los Angeles freeway, waiting to see what would happen next.

Most of the time, even all these years later, when I tell people about what happened, I know where their minds go: cop shows like *Law & Order*, slasher movies like *Scream*. Sometimes they'll mention these titles themselves, won't even try to hide it. But they know the murder wasn't committed by some masked man, some stranger wearing a black hood. So, they'll usually offer another reference, like the early 2000s mother-daughter melodrama *White Oleander*, starring Michelle Pfeiffer as a troubled and beautiful mother incarcerated for murder.

I'd love to hear your thoughts on Orange Is the New Black, said a co-worker once after I told her at happy hour.

I've never seen it, I said, swirling the ice around in my glass. She seemed genuinely surprised.

Others have asked me if interrogation rooms really have mirrored windows, if I really had to sit in the backseat of a cop car, if I ever had to talk to my mom through glass with an old school telephone.

I'm sorry, it's just, it's kind of like the movies, they usually say. *People must ask you stuff like that all the time.*

I think back to the only part of the *Scream* franchise I've ever seen—the opening in *Scream 4*, the one where the blonde kills the other blonde because it's really *Stab 7*.

It's been done to death, I think. Still, I smile and nod, answer their questions, no matter how intrusive, no matter what bad thoughts they conjure in me.

Nick painted his face bright white with thick costume makeup, blood dripping red like the balloons he held in his hands. It all started when the movie remake of Stephen King's novel, *It,* was released. I never would have guessed my brother would be interested in cosplay, but when he posted the first photo of himself dressed up on Instagram, I thought back to one of his old Halloween costumes in 2010, just two years after Betty died. He wore a form-fitting, long-sleeve brown shirt with a laminated badge around his neck that read *Dexter Morgan, Forensics Examiner.* His girlfriend at the time wore only layers of Saranwrap with fake blood spattered across the clear plastic.

He's Dexter and I'm one of his victims! she explained, gesturing to the blood as they proudly posed for photos. Betty had loved that show, used to record episodes on the DVR during its first two seasons. I wondered if Nick's girlfriend knew about Betty, about the murder, about Mom. I smiled and took the photo, pushing away a bad thought.

Nick's first popular costume was Pennywise. He wore clown clothes and shoes, caked his face in white. He trained his lips to curl back, reveal the sharp teeth that could rip off little Georgie's arm in a rainy sewer drain. The attention to detail was impressive, professional even. He'd spent hours perfecting his look, smoothing makeup over his big, fake forehead, dabbing blood on his face and clothes in just the right places.

The closest I got to horror since Betty's death was in college, when I watched the original two seasons of David Lynch's *Twin Peaks* in one weekend. It was my first real *binge* since the days of watching *Law & Order* on the couch with Mom and Betty. My obsession with the show was unexpected—I usually hated stories about murder. But I loved the show because it was silly but not stupid, spooky but not gory. It was one of the only crime shows I could watch without covering my eyes. It offered a unique portrait of teenagers—not much older than I was when Betty died—grappling with the trauma and grief of a murder in a small town. I saw myself in many of the characters, even the adults. I admired them because their grief was loud and absurd all the time: Laura's mother screaming and crying hysterically, her father dancing with the now-iconic photo of his dead daughter, her best friend searching for the truth about the crime. I watched those scenes and thought: exactly. When you lose someone you love, especially when the loss feels like the stuff of horror movies, you want to scream at the top of your lungs. You want to remember what it was like to look at their face instead of a photo. You want to find out why any of this ever had to happen.

But Nick was different. He loved scary movies, seemingly all of a sudden. I used to like them when I was younger, and I'd even convinced Betty to pay for a friend and me to see the ultra-gory *Final Destination 3* at the movie theater just two years before she died. I told Nick he looked like Mom when he wore too much makeup. He let out a weak laugh, though he hadn't spoken to her in years. I still talked and wrote to her, updated her on his life.

He's into this dress-up thing, I tried to explain on one of our phone calls. Most of the time, he and his friends would dress up as characters from movies and shows like *Harry Potter* and *Stranger Things,* but nothing was as memorable or as popular as Pennywise. He spent more time improving his design, from the details of his outfit to the way he moved. At a convention, he even took a photo with the real actors from the movie, asking us to believe, just for a moment, that this was the closest he'd ever come to a real horror scene.

I wondered about Nick's interest in stories about the act of killing, often in the most brutal ways. Once, he posted pictures of himself dressed as Otis Driftwood from Rob Zombie's gruesome slashers, *House of 1000 Corpses* and *The Devil's Rejects.* Unlike *It,* there were no childish or playful elements to these movies or their characters. Driftwood, supposedly based on Charles Manson, reached peak popularity in the early 2000s when I was in middle school.

It was the first time many of us had unsupervised access to the internet at home. Kids would brag about the grotesque things they'd seen on rotten.com, whose tagline claimed it was *an archive of disturbing illustration.* The site was controversial for its collection of explicit, unfiltered content, from photos of autopsies to close-ups of celebrities' dead bodies to obscene sex acts. The rumor was that rotten.com, along with other dark corners of the internet, contained endless information about the Manson Family murders, like uncensored photos of the victims. This made young people around me even more obsessed with Zombie's retelling. One of Driftwood's most famous lines was based on what Charles "Tex" Watson announced at Roman Polanski's home right before the murders began: *I am the devil, and I'm here to do the devil's work.*

I had spent years running away from anything that might remind me of the murder, but it seemed like Nick had run in the opposite direction. He had immersed himself in blood and guts, and I didn't want to judge him for it. Every year, he attends Halloween Horror Nights at Universal Studios, an elaborate annual celebration of the horror genre. The park's cast members dress as zombies or murder victims or movie monsters in bloodied sets themed after horror movies and their tropes. Cast members even wield fake weapons like knives and bats, surrounding guests and chasing them around the park.

I never asked Nick what he saw in Betty's room that night, what it was like when the 9-1-1 operator asked him to place his hands on her wounded neck. I never wanted to make him uncomfortable, cross a line, take his memories and make them my own, as so many others had done with mine. I thought of my own obsessive behavior, mainly how I changed my hair constantly like Mom used to do. I'd bleached it, given myself highlights with a butter knife, dyed it jet black and then fire engine red, cut my own bangs with kitchen scissors, thinned it out with shears. I'd done it all with the help of YouTube, never seeking out professional hair care. Maybe Nick was doing his own version of the same thing when he put those wigs on, painted his face.

When I scroll through my Instagram feed and see him standing there, covered in fake blood, I try not to think about what he looked like with his white shirt smeared red while we waited for police to arrive. Instead, I imagine him working with his tools, his brushes, his paint, his wigs, finding ways to tell a different story—one where he doesn't have to be the one to check the pulse.

Santa Fe New Mexican
October 23, 2009

Defendant a "Time Bomb"

A Santa Fe County woman convicted of killing her mother in June is a "time bomb just waiting to go off again" who deserves the maximum 15-year sentence for her crime, a state district judge said Thursday.

In a rambling statement before the judge sentenced her, A.D. repeatedly said she wasn't responsible for 68-year-old Betty R.'s brutal stabbing death in the early morning hours of May 6, 2008, at the home they shared in Nambé. Her mother was her best friend, she said.

"I'm convinced that in your mind you're convinced you didn't commit this crime," Judge Michael Vigil told A.D. "The underlying issue that brought this murder about is your mental illness and your inability to manage that illness. I need to lock you up for as long as I can."

A.D. told the judge that her mother's death was a heinous crime. "My mother did not deserve to be attacked in her bed (and) brutally murdered in front of her grandchildren," she said. "Me killing my mother, it's not a possibility. I went from soccer mom to Charles Manson overnight? No."

When I started writing about the murder, I wrote about it the same way I spoke about it: with uncertainty. I realized how I must have sounded when I said things like, *My grandma was murdered, and my mom went to prison for the crime.* Or, *My mom went to prison after my grandma was murdered.* Once I started sending work out for publication, I noticed a trend: editors would change the areas of ambiguity around whether I thought Mom killed Betty. They'd change titles, change URLs, change sentences to reflect the certainty they must have felt.

When I would press them about these changes, they'd offer something about tightening the prose, the need for more concise language. Once, when I emailed an editor to ask that he change a URL to one of my essays because it said something like my-mother-killed-my-grandma, I never received a response. They got my essay, posted it on the homepage with a generic image of a crime scene closed off with caution tape. Sometimes

I thought about what Mom might say if she ever got out and read what I'd written. I'd spent all these years on the phone with her, being the only family member who'd pick up, telling her I believed her.

I know you didn't do it, Mom, I'd say. *I was there.* More performing. More pretending.

A few nights after my twenty-second birthday, a classmate from grad school drunkenly told me I should create a podcast about Betty's murder.

I just think that your, you know, story would be great for something like that, she explained.

I'd moved to New York for an MFA program with the goal of *investigating* and writing about what happened in 2008. I hadn't known what an MFA program was until one of my undergraduate professors looked me in the eye in office hours and said, *You have memoir written all over you.* She turned out to be the Ms. Graham of college, a mentor who saw me in ways others couldn't. During my first semester of graduate school, the true crime podcast *Serial* had been released, detailing the death of Hae Min Lee, an eighteen-year-old high school student from Baltimore who'd been strangled to death in 1999. Her ex-boyfriend, Adnan Syed, was convicted of first-degree murder in 2000 and sentenced to life in prison. Now, new details had emerged from the podcast, causing many to question whether Syed was truly guilty.

With new episodes airing weekly, it felt like everyone with a smartphone was obsessed with finding out what had happened in Baltimore all those years ago. I couldn't escape it: on Twitter, I scrolled through endless conversations about the podcast, how *amazing* and *addictive* it was, and in my nonfiction writing classes, my peers would discuss its creators' incredible storytelling, how we should all strive to match the unwavering commitment to telling the truth.

At first, my approach to my own investigation was meticulous: I wrote down every detail I could possibly remember, organized files for everything. I pushed my memory to its limits, forced myself to get it all down, even the parts that hurt the most, the ones that brought me to tears alone at my laptop. I studied my copies of the police reports and newspaper articles and the transcripts from the trial like never before, with a precision I couldn't explain. I'd become obsessed. I wanted the details, all of them, anything that could help me say what happened—because I wanted them to help me understand *why* it happened.

The whole point, I had started to think, was to turn everything into *story,* something beautiful. To take what had been crushing me on the inside and finally get it out on the page. I read and reread passages from Virginia Woolf's *Moments of Being,* and I wrote my favorite quote down and taped it to the wall in my studio apartment: *It is only by putting it into words that I make it whole; this wholeness means that it has lost its power to hurt me; it gives me, perhaps because by doing so I take away the pain, a great delight to put the severed parts together.*

I soon learned that most readers did not come to my story with hopes that I'd found ways to make it hurt me less. They came to my story, a story of murder, hungry for sensation, the way a viewer comes to a scary movie, eager with one hand in a bucket of buttery popcorn. When they asked me questions, it was like our dusty workshop classroom became another interrogation room. One morning in particular, a woman in class critiqued my workshop submission by saying what she would have done if she were me.

Well, to be honest, I would have gotten out of bed earlier, she said. Some nodded, others looked down at the table. *I don't care how old you are. Teenager or not, if someone is being murdered in your house, you get up.*

I could feel all the other eyes on me as I sunk down in my chair, cheeks flushed red with that same guilt I'd been fighting off each day and night for years now. Some mornings it felt like there might as well have been a bright light and a mirror staring back at me while the students in my workshop discussed my writing.

I shouldn't have been surprised by how many writers, especially those around my age, only had one frame of reference for thinking about my work: crime TV. Most millennials had grown up binge watching *SVU* and *CSI* or losing sleep after Lifetime's *Unsolved Mysteries* marathons just as I had. Some even had conscious memories of the OJ Simpson car chase and months-long trial.

Many of their lives had been shaped by what they saw on the televisions and, later, the computers in their homes. They, like me, had grown up with stories and images of violence at their fingertips. Even I had thought of *SVU*'s Detective Olivia Benson when I sat helpless in the interrogation rooms that night. When they read scenes about detectives questioning witnesses and looking for weapons, their only point of entry was the entertainment they'd spent hours of their lives consuming. Once, in a workshop where I'd submitted a piece about giving the dispatcher the wrong address, an older male colleague said, *You said it yourself: you watched* Law & Order *every day. Didn't that prepare you?*

> Now, some people would say why would a 15-year-old not know what to say [to the 9-1-1 dispatcher]? First of all, she's scared to death. And while she's 15 and somewhat mature on the stand, she's still, I think, a scared little girl.
>
> —Prosecution's Closing Argument, *State v. A.D.*, 2009

In grad school, podcasts like *Serial* complicated my experience of sharing my own story, too. Suddenly, true crime stories were everywhere, establishing themselves as something new, something different from those cable shows about fictionalized murders and abductions. New podcasts were popping up to tell more stories of more murders that had slipped through the cracks in small-town America, relying on archival audio clips from the cases and even new interviews with key people who'd been involved.

Just before I moved to New York, a major cable network had approached Mom and asked her to appear in an episode of one of their shows about women who commit murder. They wanted to interview her from inside the prison, depict her everyday life, ask her questions about the night it happened. The show followed the same formula as the others like it—if you'd seen one, you'd seen them all—and featured interviews with people close to the case, like friends of the victim or journalists who'd reported on the crime when the story first broke. Mom declined. The same year, an article appeared online: "The Women Murderers Behind Bars in New Mexico," it was titled, and it featured a slideshow of pictures of Mom and her friends.

Check out their mugshots, it said.

Living in a world obsessed with murder was suffocating. People loved to ask me if I'd ever seen *Snapped* or the recent Netflix documentary *Making a Murderer*. I just wanted my actual trauma to exist apart from all those cheap tropes, all those dramatic reenactments that had gotten it so wrong. I wanted people to know how unglamorous it was when the murder was real, not invented or embellished in some writer's room or TV studio. How there were no Detective Bensons in this story, no sensitive-yet-powerful police officer to comfort me when I sat shivering in the back of a police car like I was the one who'd done something wrong. How there was no long-faced ghoul terrorizing my neighborhood with a knife, no posse of beautiful women running around trying to find out who was hiding behind the mask all along.

In my apartment in New York, I was still afraid of the dark, so I slept with twelve feet of white Christmas lights strung up against the wall beside my bed. It was then, at the age of twenty-two, that I finally had my first real dream about Betty. It took place, like all of the nightmares before it, inside our old house where she died. The difference was that Mom and Betty were both alive. There were no screams or bloodstains.

In the dream, the two of them lay in Betty's old bed together as a small dog slept at the foot of the bed on a cushion. I opened the door to walk into the room, and a light beamed across the bed from behind me as the dog jumped up and barked at me. I couldn't see Mom because she was hidden beneath the blankets, but I could hear her. She was there. I could see Betty now as the light shone against her. She was lying in the bed in her long-sleeve green nightgown, looking how she used to when she went to bed after one of our TV shows had ended or one of our arguments had just begun. She lifted her head up, turned to me, and said, *Can you turn off the light?*

I startled awake, sat in my bed looking at the string of lights glowing on the wall for a long time. I wondered how it had taken almost seven years for me to find her again. For the first time, it wasn't a nightmare. There was no blood. No screaming. I wanted to know what had changed, why I was never able to see her that way before. Betty wanted me to sleep in the dark. She gave me permission. I unplugged the lights from the wall, got back into bed, and closed my eyes, hoping to see her again.

The summer after my first year of grad school, I attended a writing conference at a small college in the Pacific Northwest. I was eager to meet new writers, find new readers for my work. My workshop instructor was not my first choice, but I was excited to work with him anyway because his name appeared on the cover of so many books I'd seen at Strand that year. On the first night of the conference, I purchased several of those books with what money I'd made at my work-study job compiling research and photocopying archival documents for one of the deans at the university.

This would be just what I needed to finish my project, to write everything down, to discover the truth. But over the course of the conference, I started to notice things, like how aside from the instructor, there was only one man in the classroom, how this shaped our conversations about the things the women chose to write about. I noted the instructor's reoccurring use of the statement, *This subject matter is just inherently uninteresting to me,* to preface his comments about many of the women's workshop submissions about childhood, body image, divorce, or sexuality.

When it was finally my turn to be workshopped, toward the end of the week-long conference, I tried not to be nervous. After all, I was in an MFA program where I shared personal material about the murder with my classmates every two weeks, still trying to numb myself to the comments from peers who could not separate the person I was in the room from the person I was on the page. The instructor wasted no time dissecting the twenty-five pages of prose I submitted, saying he liked the part when the detectives bought Nick and me McDonald's breakfast as we sat in the police station wondering if we would ever go home again. He thought it was sort of *funny*. Soon, though, the conversation turned, like they often did, from the actions and emotions of the narrator to a discussion, an evaluation, of me as a person.

The instructor started to dissect the outfit I was wearing: the Taylor Swift shirt I'd gotten at her concert earlier that summer, even the white Converse sneakers on my feet. He said he was surprised that out of everyone in the room, I was the one who wrote the manuscript about the murder. Because of the clothes I wore to class every day, he explained, having known me for four days. It struck him that I was the same age as his daughter, so young, writing all this darkness about a brutal murder.

He wanted everyone in the room to know that he couldn't imagine *the murder manuscript* coming from someone like me because people who wore the clothes I wore were not the kind of people who have experienced pain. He said he would believe me—my prose, he corrected himself—more if I were wearing a Lana Del Rey shirt instead of a Taylor Swift one because *that girl, Lana, now she's a sad one, she can get pretty dark.* I tried to ask him to stop, saying, *I think this is a little inappropriate,* because nobody else in the workshop before me had to listen to the instructor comment on their clothing, their appearance, their age. I started to think of taking off my clothes in the interrogation room, but I had to stop myself. *No. Don't.*

Two people tried to defend me, to stop it.

I don't think a woman's clothes should have anything to do with what she writes, said one classmate, and he hissed, *This isn't really a feminist issue.* It was the same thing he said during another woman's workshop three days earlier, but that time, we'd gotten through the whole manuscript without talking about what the author wore to class.

After I ran out of the room crying, to go to the bathroom to find some tissues or a place to hide, one of the women in class, a mother, tried to speak to the instructor in the hall about his professionalism. I overheard it all. He said, *How dare you,* and told her that she was probably very good at her job, at being a middle school teacher, but that this was his job and he knew what he was doing. When I returned to the classroom with bloodshot eyes, he said, *I guess we should address the elephant in the room,* as if I were making a big deal out of something that was completely normal, funny even.

He explained he was trying to provide me, and the rest of the students, with a metaphor about my prose, that the sentences were too calm when they should have more explicitly matched the terror of what I'd experienced. He said I wrote too perfectly, my lines too clean and poised. He thought it would make more sense if the sentences mirrored the trauma, by being as chaotic as it *must have been, as you claim,* to hide in my room while all of it was going on.

It's as if the prose is wearing a Taylor Swift shirt, he said, proud of himself. *A disguise. A mask.* He didn't mean for his metaphor to offend me, he assured us all. It might be hard for people to believe I was really there when the murder happened if the sentences I used to describe it were too calm, too clean, as if trying to hide something.

After class finally ended, one of the two women who tried to interject reported the instructor to the conference administrators. Later, I sat in an office answering questions, or different versions of a single question, fluffed up to alter it slightly from the last. The man doing the asking told me that the instructor would be leaving the conference early, although it was already coming to an end, and would not be asked to come back again.

Back at my apartment, before I even unpacked my suitcase, I pulled out my collection of transcripts from the trial. On my bookshelf, I had five spiral-bound books, organized by the five days of the trial. I knew these books better than any text I'd ever studied in school, any favorite book I'd read and reread, and instantly, I flipped to the page where, in the book labeled *DAY 3*, my testimony began.

The first page was marked with the date, June 17, 2009, just two months before my senior year of high school would begin. I'd combed through the transcripts countless times before, searching for answers to my questions, almost always coming up short. But this time was different: after the humiliation of the writing conference, I'd begun to question myself. How many others had doubted my trauma? How many others, like the men I used to tell all about that night on dates, had thought I'd just made it all up, decided I didn't seem sad or damaged enough for it to be true?

I turned to the transcripts one last time for proof, for validation, to remind myself that, yes, it was me up there on the stand at sixteen. It was me talking about the screaming and the blood. It was me who stood in the doorway, found my mother in a blood stained shirt. I existed. My pain was real. I took out a bright green highlighter, marked and circled, turned back to reread some sections again, like the first time the attorney asked me to talk about the screams.

Reading the transcripts again, I learned things. I learned that during the investigation, no blood had been found on the front doorknob, although Mom ran out into the front yard after I found her in Betty's room, taking the phone with her while I went to get Nick from his room down the hall. No blood had been found on the phone either. And nobody had ever tested either one, not the doorknob or the phone, with luminol, to see if blood had been wiped off at some point that night.

There were other things, too, that made me sick when I read them. Like that most of the time, when you stab someone, their blood will get all over you, on your face and in your hair, maybe even in your eyes. Or that when there's a struggle, when the victim fights back, they end up with their attacker's skin, their DNA, under their fingernails. But nobody ever checked

Mom's hair, and nobody ever tested Betty's fingernails. They just saw the blood on Mom and wrote down what I said—how I'd walked in and seen her there, standing over something on the floor of Betty's room.

Case closed, they must have said. *That was easy.*

I sat and read the transcripts for a long time, thinking how hard it had been to answer those questions back then, to be forced to recall any horrifying detail on command. It was painful to see my old self documented that way in all those pages, an awkward teenager stumbling over certain words, saying *like* in every other sentence and laughing nervously as the jury stared. Try to please everyone, try not to take up too much space. Don't be wrong. Don't mess this up again. I even asked the judge if I was allowed to say bad words when the attorney asked me to repeat what Nick had said to the 9-1-1 dispatcher. I should have been out with friends, driving to the beach or the mall, obsessing about normal teenager things.

The administrative office at the writing conference, like the classroom at the writing conference, like maybe all writing classrooms, had become just another interrogation room. Another courtroom. A place to answer the same questions over and over, to be reminded that nothing I could say would ever be right. A place to sit helplessly, waiting for the pain to go away, while other people kept asking me to prove what the screams really sounded like.

My boyfriend Nathan and I were on a road trip when we decided to try listening to the *Serial* podcast. It had been over a year since it was first released, and the conversation around it had mostly died down. A few other true crime podcasts had started gaining traction since then, like *My Favorite Murder,* the most offensive title I'd heard yet. Lately, I'd been thinking about why these shows had become so successful, why they were so addictive to their audiences.

I assumed it all started with *Serial,* and I wanted to know why. I wondered where the creators of the podcasts found out about the crimes they covered, how they got all the documents that related to the case, how they tracked down certain details, big and small, that law enforcement had apparently missed. Some part of me also worried that, with so many of these shows popping up, someday I might go online and see people tweeting about some new podcast episode about Betty's death, theorizing about what went wrong that night. It was nauseating to think of anyone ever referring to Betty's murder as their *favorite.*

It was Thanksgiving break, and we were in a black truck we rented outside of LaGuardia Airport, on our way to North Carolina, where Craig still lived. Nathan and I had just celebrated our first anniversary and decided to take a road trip. I hadn't been back to North Carolina in years, but Craig and I stayed in touch once we reconnected while I was in college. We even saw each other in person a few times when he visited his family in Florida near campus. Nathan and I had met when we first started our MFA program, but we never really talked at school.

Although we had both lived in New York for the same amount of time, our first real conversation happened in Portland, on the last night of the writing conference we both attended. We exchanged small talk as we sat in the back row of a big lecture hall, waiting to hear a talk about writing the body. He leaned over to ask me if I'd heard about the woman whose outfit had been workshopped by a male instructor in one of the classes. At first, I was embarrassed, like this was *me* now. My identity. I guessed everyone at the conference knew what had happened or at least someone else's version of what happened. But Nathan's tone wasn't cruel or mocking, and he didn't seem interested in petty gossip. He seemed genuinely angry. He didn't think someone like that should be allowed to teach anywhere.

No matter how successful a writer is, he shouldn't be allowed to talk about a student's appearance.

That was me, I said, my face burning red, and he looked shocked, embarrassed, like he'd said something stupid and wished he could take it back. He apologized, saying he didn't want to make me feel uncomfortable or make me think about the instructor any more than I probably already had.

I'm really sorry that happened to you, he said, and the lecture started.

That night, I ran into him again, at the final gathering for the writers to say goodbye before we all checked out of our dorms and left the following morning. I couldn't wait to get out of there. Nathan and I sat under a big tree in the school's main courtyard, where we stayed talking for hours. At first, I was nervous he'd only want to talk about what had happened in the workshop, but he didn't even bring it up. He didn't ask me any questions, didn't want me to prove how bad it had made me feel.

Talking to him was different. I didn't have to tell him gory details of my life to make him want to listen to me, to convince him that I was worth talking to. We spoke about writing, about his poems, which were about his family, mostly his dad, and his hometown. We spoke about living in New York, how we had both been born in warmer climates—me in Florida and he in California—and we hated the city snow with equal passion. He asked me if I planned to live there forever after graduation, if I had hopes to pursue a job in publishing or try to get a book of my own out in the world.

I knew that he already knew about the murder because he'd heard me share some of my work at readings on campus. He told me that he liked my writing, thought I had an important story to tell, one that could open people's minds, challenge them to have more empathy. When he looked at me, I felt seen for the first time in so long. I loved his smile, and I clung to his laughter while we spoke, eager to hear it again and again. A few months after we got back to New York and our second year of grad school began, we went out on our first date. Soon after, we moved in together, to an apartment at the top of Manhattan with more night lights than rooms, where he held me and rubbed my back whenever I woke up sweat soaked from another nightmare.

By the time we drove to North Carolina the following year, he already knew the saga of Mom and Craig, how it spanned across multiple houses and states and years. In the rental truck, we started playing the first episode of *Serial.* I felt a quick jolt of shock during the opening, stunned by the familiar sound of a call from prison.

This is a Global-Tel Link prepaid call from Adnan Syed, an inmate at a Maryland correctional facility.

It reminded me of the one I heard every time Mom called me: *This call is from an inmate at a state correctional facility*. That sound wasn't something I'd ever thought twice about because it had just become part of my life. When Mom called, I answered by pressing one to accept the call. It felt wrong to hear that sound in this context. It made me feel gross, like I was eavesdropping on someone else's phone call like the guards do, looking in on someone else's life—without their permission.

In her opening remarks about the purpose of *Serial* and how the story came to be, the host Sarah Koenig included a slight disclaimer, explaining that she was not a detective or a private investigator.

I'm not even a crime reporter, she went on to say. I found it fascinating: this highly successful podcast, which had broken records and won awards, was simply rooted in curiosity. I wanted to hate it, but there was something so human, so real about how forthcoming Koenig was from the start.

We finished the entire first season during that trip. Sometimes we had to stop, turn it off, and regroup because I got too upset by some of the disturbing details. Some parts of the story made my stomach hurt, made me want to cry for everyone involved, or reminded me too much of my own experiences—talking to cops, looking for answers, coming out from a deep, dark rabbit hole empty-handed.

I cringed, especially, at the inclusion of recorded interrogations, police interviews of people closely involved with the case. There was something almost voyeuristic about those clips. I imagined how I'd feel knowing other people were listening to recordings of my own interrogations from that night in 2008—how it would feel like just another violation on top of all the others that had happened over the years. It was bad enough when the jury had to listen to the tape of my 9-1-1 call, my voice shaking over the line as I somehow sounded even younger than I was at the time. There were other parallels, too, like loose ends in the investigation, concerns about errors the police and Syed's attorney might have made on the case.

At times, as we listened, it was too much to take, too painful to be reminded how many questions in my own life remained unanswered. How unfair it was that others lived like this, too. But the sense of curiosity—a desire to *know*—at the center of this long and tragic story of violence was intriguing. It was clear from the first episode that Koenig was not interested in trying to maintain any sort of journalistic or investigative distance as she reported. She was a real person, who, when faced with the facts and the questions about this very real, very complex murder case, became emotionally invested. She even developed a sort of friendship with Syed through their conversations. She wasn't there to stir up old trauma and comment on it on her radio show. This was something else. She recognized the magnitude of what a murder could do, what it had already done, and what it could continue to do even though fifteen years had already gone by.

Serial was similar to the various forms of crime as entertainment I'd consumed in my young life in that it hooked its audience and made us obsessed—but it differed in its conclusion. At the end, Koenig sat us down one last time to let us know that there would be no resolutions here. Maybe there would never be. In the final episode, she went back to the beginning, to when she first heard about the case.

Certainty, one way or the other, seemed so attainable. We just needed to get the right documents, spend enough time, talk to the right people, find [the] alibi. . . . We all thought, how hard can this possibly be?

After the final episode, I stared out the window and thought about this question, about the things many of us are left to wonder after the arrest is made, the evidence is filed away, and the case is closed. How many of us go on wondering, asking, searching?

I was reminded of all the times I'd been asked whether or not I thought Mom actually did it, if there were ever any doubts in my mind or questions about other possibilities.

You were there. You should know.

Or how I myself told Mom, *I was there. I know you didn't.*

When I force myself to dig and dig and dig to try to remember something from that night, it can start to feel like my mind is playing tricks on me. Maybe I've thought about something so hard, so many times that I've actually changed it, started to remember it differently now. I know I can't reach back into the past and move things around, make them make sense.

Flip on the light switch in Betty's room.

Give the operator the right address.

Get out of bed as soon as I hear that sound.

By my second year of grad school, I had accidentally become the poster girl for prison. When all of your classes are nonfiction workshops, everyone around you knows the intimate details of your life. Even the worst parts, the things you used to live in shame about, the things you tried to hide. Somehow, those things become your identity after years of not wanting to be defined by them. After sharing my writing around the city, publishing essays online, I felt visible for the first time. I didn't walk around school feeling ashamed, like I had to be someone else. The truth was out in the open. People knew about the murder. They knew where Mom was. I felt like my trauma had brought me into existence, proved that I was alive, surviving.

I was invited to speak on panels about parental incarceration, asked to introduce events about the criminal justice system. I participated in an arts show for children of incarcerated parents. I hosted an open mic for formerly incarcerated men and women at a halfway house. For a while, I felt empowered, felt important. My suffering hadn't been for nothing. It was helping me make a difference, even a small one. But constantly pushing against the common narratives about *justice,* about *crime* had a price. I had already been writing about my trauma but talking about it was different. It took a special kind of toll on me, exhausted me in a new way. I'd get hives on my neck and back, endure random bouts of nausea and hours-long migraines. I felt exposed, poked, and prodded. But I kept saying yes because other people seemed to care. They made me feel like sharing what had happened was somehow worth the pain of reliving it.

That was how I ended up teaching a creative writing class for teen girls at Rikers Island every Tuesday. That was how I ended up willingly crossing through the metal detectors I hated. That was how I ended up watching a guard slap a young woman in a jumpsuit like the one Mom wore. That was how I ended up in class with Dee, a student who was just a little older than I was at the time of the murder. Dee called me ugly every single class. She told me she hated me. She said my clothes were stupid. My short hair made me look like a boy. I wasn't very smart for a goddamn motherfucking teacher.

Why are you so fucking ugly? she asked. *I hate you and this stupid fucking poem.*

Don't you ever want to quit? one of the other staff members asked, sighing. *This place, you know? It's crazy sometimes.* The girls we taught were just teenagers, most of them wrapped up with gangs or much older boyfriends at a young age. Most of them didn't share why they were in jail, but the few that did were charged with attempted murder. Aggravated battery. Armed robbery.

One day during class, Dee said she wanted to ask me a question. Everyone else perked up, eager to see what she was going to do this time.

Well, I don't know why I'm so ugly, I said before she could even ask. *I guess I was just born that way.*

No, she said. *I want to know why you're here. Why do you come in here every week? Why do you give a shit?*

You really want to know? The other girls put down their pens, papers stopped rustling. The room went quiet.

My mom is in prison, I said. *For murdering my grandma. My brother and I were in the house. I still talk to her. I'm the only one who does.*

I told her how Mom had started writing poetry, that it made her feel better to get her feelings out on the page. I didn't know what I expected Dee to say. I thought she might make fun of me, laugh it off. Boohoo, she might say. Who cares? I expected to feel that familiar nausea, that rash creeping up my chest and arms. The shame. But Dee sat down in the plastic chair beside me, looked me in the eyes. She said, *Before I got in here, my grandma raised me. She's the only one who ever cared about me. She got me what I needed when she could. Shoes I wanted. A jacket for winter. Fed me. She gave a fuck. Nobody ever gave a fuck, you know what I mean?*

Yeah, I said. *I do.* I held back tears, looked around the room. Almost every student was teary-eyed, faces shiny under the florescent lights.

And you know, you're not that *ugly,* said Dee, half-smiling. Then the guards came in and told us class was over. The girls lined up for count, and I stood up and packed my clear backpack.

The following Tuesday, Dee ran up to me at the start of class.

We all wrote letters to your mama, she said. *Every one of us.* She got permission from the guard and handed me a stack of folded paper.

She told me I could read them if I wanted.

Your daughter taught me how to write this, one of them said.

Your daughter is real smart.

I hope you know how good of a daughter you got, wrote Dee. *You got a really special daughter.*

I mailed them to Mom, but they got returned before they reached her. They were stuffed into my apartment mailbox, a rubber band wrapped tightly around them. Some of the pages were ripped, some letters were missing. *NO INMATE TO INMATE CONTACT* was written in bold red ink. I hugged them to my chest, locked them in my filing cabinet. I never told the girls they got sent back.

After I finished grad school, I applied for a job teaching English at a business college in Manhattan. I'd taught at Rikers, and then, I'd gotten a fellowship to teach a nonfiction workshop my last semester before I graduated. It seemed like everyone in the MFA program was either teaching, working in publishing, or moving on to get another graduate degree. I didn't know what else to do. A friend had helped me with my application materials, and although I felt completely unqualified, I'd somehow gotten an interview. Waiting outside the department chair's office, I felt like a fraud.

There were some moments I couldn't experience without thinking about everything that had happened before. I wondered, before the murder, or immediately after, could I have imagined myself even going to college? I thought about what Betty might have said if I could tell her I might *teach* college. English. Her favorite subject. If I could tell her that all the books she'd given me led me to this moment. Our trips to Borders, the lists of titles she'd written out for me.

But then I'd think: wait, I'm not smart enough for this. I missed too much school growing up, moving from place to place. I didn't even do well on the SAT. I can't take tests. I have panic attacks. I don't even know how to fall asleep. What would I be able to teach these students? What am I doing thinking I deserve a job like this? My mother was in prison, my grandmother was dead. Nobody in my family had ever done anything like this. I'm not like the other people in these halls. Would I have even gotten here if I hadn't spent these years writing about the murder? Would anyone have thought I was a good writer if it was about anything else? Were people like me supposed to be in these kinds of rooms?

I imagined the department chair as another kind of interrogator. Dr. Bradley would ask me questions I didn't know how to answer, and I'd hate myself for getting them wrong. I'd leave feeling disappointed, probably cry on the way home. I'd be reminded that I didn't belong anywhere. But she was warm and welcoming, and she made me feel important. She didn't ask me to prove why I deserved to be there, didn't make me feel like a phony or a failure. Instead, she told me about someone in her life who died unexpectedly. She gestured to the framed photo on her desk, and we both started crying. She told me my work interested her, that talking about trauma and loss was important. She told me that most people weren't willing to face those kinds of things, that she admired the way I was telling my story.

I got the job, I imagined myself saying to Betty as I rode home on the subway.

Months later, my teaching had to be observed and evaluated for the department's annual review. A senior faculty member came to my classroom, sat in the back and took notes during class. I was teaching an introductory composition class themed around injustice. We watched documentaries about incarceration, read articles in the *Marshall Project*. I asked students to write rhetorical analyses of representations of prison in the media. It had been deeply rewarding, if a little triggering. During the first week, a student came up to me after class and asked me if my mom really *killed someone*.

When I tell people about that, I say I blacked out. I was so shocked by the question, that a college freshman would ask me such a thing. When I think back to it, I try to imagine the look on my face, but I can't see the moment. I don't know what I said, what anyone could say to a question like that. Starting the following week, he would stay after class, share his work with me. I was hesitant at first, but then, we started talking. He told me about his own struggles, his own grief. He said knowing what I'd been through helped him, that it made the class feel like a safe place to be. He apologized if his question had crossed a line.

After the observation, I had a meeting with Dr. Bradley to go over my evaluation. The previous day, I'd gotten a call from Mom. I still talked to her as much as I could, sending cards and letters when I had time. She knew I was busy, but I still dropped everything when she called. She always wanted to hear about Nick, who hadn't talked to her in years now. I would update her on his life, if he was dating, what he was doing for work. She had been feeling sick lately, and although she was over fifty now, she had started bleeding. The guards taunted her, told her it was just her period coming back.

Something is really wrong, she said, and finally, after months of trying to see a doctor, she found out she was right.

Colon cancer, she said. I froze. She had a tumor in her intestine, and she was going to need surgery to remove it. I put the phone on speaker and started googling. *How bad is colon cancer?* I typed. I found out colorectal cancer was divided into stages: 3A, 3B, and 3C.

What stage is it? I asked Mom, reading off a medical website. She said we wouldn't find out until after the surgery. I couldn't help but break down crying, and Mom got frustrated.

Stop, she said. *Please. I can't deal with that now.*

Sorry. I have to go anyway, I said. *I have an important meeting tomorrow.*

After we hung up, I paced around my apartment crying, waiting for Nathan to get home from work. The next morning, I went into Dr. Bradley's office for my meeting. I used concealer to hide my puffy eyes, pretend I hadn't been up all night crying. That I hadn't been doubled over on the bathroom tile, dry heaving during what felt like an hours-long panic attack. Before we even started discussing the evaluation, Dr. Bradley asked how my day was going so far. Then it started again: the tears. Full on sobbing. Heavy breathing. I physically could not contain myself. I was shaking, inconsolable.

I'm so sorry, I said again and again. I felt like I was shouting. *I just found out my mom has cancer.* Dr. Bradley paused.

Don't apologize, she said. *We don't need to meet about this today. If I found out my mom had cancer, I wouldn't be here right now.*

Really? I asked, trying to calm down. *But you're my boss. This is my first real job.* She closed the folder on the table, took a deep breath. She gave me permission to go home, lie down.

Take care of yourself, she said. *Will you do that?*

In the visiting room, Mom asked the guard to give me a maxi pad. It was thick and white, nondescript. No brand I'd ever heard of.

We ain't got Always with Wings in here, the guard said, laughing.

I was twenty-five, but I felt like some dumb teenager, getting my period at the worst time. I wasn't allowed to have my purse, couldn't even wear a belt into the visiting room. It was the first time I'd seen Mom in seven years, since my first year of college, and now, I had red splotches crawling up my neck from the guard's joke.

My period had always been a problem. Painful, unruly. I'd never know when it was coming. In high school, I sat doubled over at my desk, face down on my notebook. Before the murder, before she was gone, sometimes Mom had to pick me up early. By the time she pulled up to the school parking lot, the blood had dripped down my leg, soaked one of my socks. I hoped it wouldn't get on the Vans I'd bought with the money Betty gave me for pulling weeds in the driveway.

Good job, Betty had said with a cigarette hanging from her lips, handing Nick and me some bills she'd cashed out from the casino.

It happened again, I'd say to the answering machine. *I need to go home.* I always knew Mom could pick me up. I knew she wasn't at work, didn't have anywhere to be. She was probably at the poker room or hooked on a slot machine with some guy hitting on her. For a time, she had a job selling AVON makeup, but the tubes of lip gloss and concealer she was supposed to sell were sitting half-used on the counter in the bathroom we shared. After she picked me up, I'd get home to find I'd ruined another pair of underwear or jeans or even shoes, the stains impossible to get clean.

I'd gotten my first period on Father's Day at the casino buffet. They only served crab legs on special occasions, and Betty always had discounts because she worked there. It was better not to ask where our rural town in New Mexico sourced them. I was a picky eater. I hated butter, even the smell of it, but I loved cracking the legs open, sucking the meat out like one long limb between my teeth. I never liked using the silver cracking tools that came on the tray. They were too imprecise, too bulky. Instead, I'd break each leg in half by hand and run my fork in a straight line down the middle. Sometimes, when the meat was really stubborn, my fingers bled from the jagged red edges of the shell.

All I remember from that first period was the dress I wore—a blue Limited Too hand-me-down from one of Mom's old boyfriend's daughters—and the pain. It was the last time I'd ever wear that dress and the last Father's Day I'd ever celebrate with Craig. The next day, Betty brought home a pack of chocolate Entenmann's Doughnuts from the grocery store, and I ate half of them alone in front of the bathroom mirror, picking at my acne, trying to read the impossible instructions tucked inside the tampon box.

In the prison bathroom, I wondered, *Why now?* like a preteen in a Judy Blume novel. It was the first time since that visit in my first year of college that I'd convinced myself to visit Mom—and it was only because she had cancer. It would later turn out to be stage 3B colon cancer, the kind I shouldn't have looked up online. She was weeks away from her operation to remove the tumor and ten inches of her intestine. Seeing her face, paler than ever, and her frail body, which was now reliant on a walker to get around, I felt guilty for leaving her here alone all these years.

I blamed myself for her getting sick in the first place. Maybe loneliness caused it, I convinced myself. I couldn't bring myself to open the pad, stick it to my underwear. Instead, I shoved a wad of toilet paper in my pants and slipped the pad in my back pocket. The guard smirked at me when I returned to my chair across from Mom. We were only allowed to hug once at the beginning and once at the end of the visit. We weren't allowed to sit next to each other, per the list of rules posted on the wall. *NO CONTACT*, it read.

When I got back to New York, to my apartment with Nathan, I added the pad to a small shoebox of Mom's things I still owned. A light pink tube of lipstick, a pair of tweezers, a single earring she used to wear. I never found the matching one. I thought maybe it could have been in Betty's room since they used to share jewelry, lost after the blood was cleaned up, the caution tape torn down. Mom had missed almost everything since then, for ten years now. Prom, heartbreaks, college, grad school. But she had been there for my period, picked me up from school those days when I needed her. And now, she'd gotten me this pad. It was the only motherly act she'd been allowed to do in so long, and I wanted to keep this reminder of it forever.

After Mom's operation, our relationship was better for a while. She knew she could rely on me. She'd call me and ask for favors: call this attorney's number, send me this arts and crafts catalog, sign me up on this mailing list. She told me she loved me, sent me cards—up until the prison banned cards—about how I was the best daughter in the world. She mailed me the crochet dolls she made that were hot pink and lime green, covered in contraband glitter. She sent me poems about how beautiful I was. Told me I was the least selfish person in the world. How I'd gone through so much and remained so full of light and hope.

I felt seen by my own mother for maybe the first time. It was like being apart—and the cancer—brought us closer together. I told her she could live with Nathan and me when she got out. I'd be thirty by then, have my life together. Be ready to take care of her, help her get back on her feet. But in all honesty, it was hard to imagine that day ever coming. I didn't think of it seriously, that Mom would someday be released. That she would need somewhere to live. That I'd be the only family member in her life. That the responsibility would be on me and me alone. I sent her what money I had when I had it, making ends meet with two jobs, adjuncting at the business college and tutoring at a writing center. She bragged to her friends about me, told them I was a professor.

Back in the visiting room, she kept telling the other women who passed by in their jumpsuits that I was her daughter.

I used to look like that, she said, pointing to me.

PART FOUR Mercy

You're her only family member, said the prison official who called to tell me the news. *You have to pick her up on Friday morning.* The call was so anonymous, so nonchalant, that I'd almost thought it was a prank.

Mom was told she had another tumor—this time, in her liver—by the prison doctor. It had been less than five years since they'd removed the one from her intestine. The same parole board that denied her previous request for medical parole suddenly had a change of heart. It was two years before her release date. Nathan and I had moved to California, started a new life there. He was a PhD student, and I was teaching English at the local college. We didn't think this moment was going to come yet. But it had. We lived on campus at the college where I taught, and her parole officer would need the school's approval for her to live there.

First, I called the chair of my department, who knew about Mom's incarceration. Then, I had to meet with the university's attorney on Zoom, explain it all in a matter of minutes. I wasn't allowed to cry. I needed to be calm, professional. Keep it together.

My mom has cancer, I said.

My mom needs treatment.

Yes, my mom is in prison.

Yes, my mom is in prison for murder.

We are living through a pandemic. Prisons are not safe for sick people.

My mom's life may depend on her living here.

Yes, I can say with confidence that she is a better person now.

As soon as we got the approval, we got in Nathan's car and drove from California to New Mexico to pick Mom up. I started a GoFundMe, asked strangers if they could help me prepare for this new life. How long would she live with us, I wondered. What would she think of the way we lived? Would she like our two-bedroom apartment? Would she like California? Would she like our dog? Would she like living with Nathan? Would she even like me? On the drive, that was all I could think about. I pictured her walking out of prison, seeing me. Would my mother even like me after all these years?

When we picked her up, she didn't cry. Slowly, she floated through the parking lot like some character in a strange movie, some figment of my imagination. It was a moment I'd thought about so many times but never imagined actually happening. The guard walked her out, guiding her red prison-issued walker with her name and ID number written in silver permanent marker on the side.

I overheard the guard say, *Don't come back, okay?* and Mom nodded absentmindedly. She wore sweatpants, I think. I could go back and look at the photo Nathan took of us hugging, or of me hugging her, the watch tower in the background. The barbed wire that surrounded her for nearly thirteen years. I was crying, trying to hold her, wrap my arms around her like she was the daughter and I was the mother. Her body was stiff and lifeless, like she'd never been hugged before.

I was wearing fake Ugg boots, the light pink suede scuffed and browning, and one of the hats she crocheted for me even though I didn't like it. I wanted to like it, wanted to show her I cared about the things she did, the things she made. How she spent her time here while I waited for her to get out. I couldn't wait to show her the five Rubbermaid bins filled with hats and dolls made of purple and pink and yellow yarn, glued-on glitter shimmering somewhere in my garage.

Look at my hat, I wanted to say. *I'm here to pick you up. I'm taking you away from here. I'm always the one to rescue you.* But I just stayed quiet and watched her, tried to wipe my own tears, same as I'd always done.

I want a milkshake, she said. *There's always milkshakes on the TV commercials.* We got in the car and drove to the nearest fast-food drive-through.

In the hotel that night, she asked us to shine a flashlight over her because that's how she was used to sleeping, with the guards patrolling the prison halls while she tried to get some rest.

I don't know what it's like to sleep without it, she said. Nathan and I stayed quiet.

Mom had been living with Nathan and me for a few weeks when we talked about the murder for the first time. The first time outside of the surveillance of the prison, the first time without being recorded on a phone call. We were scrolling through Netflix, looking for something to watch. Having been gone for so long, she was overwhelmed by the advent of streaming, from Netflix to Spotify. She wondered what happened to good old-fashioned cable, DVDs, and CDs. Remote in hand, Nathan sped through the titles.

Wait, what's that? That looks good, said Mom, gesturing to the screen. It was some crime thriller, something scary I'd normally never watch.

No, I don't like watching anything with blood, I said.

Why? she asked.

Well, because, you know. The murder. Gory movies give me nightmares, I said, feeling embarrassed, confused.

Really? Mom asked. *I don't remember there being a lot of blood that night.*

Since we'd brought her home, I'd been fighting this feeling that I didn't really know Mom. That we didn't have anything in common. That maybe, in my late twenties, I was too old to connect with Mom again. We weren't affectionate with each other, hardly ever hugged or touched. One night, after I got out of the shower, she came up to me and touched my hair.

Your hair is so thick, she said. *Like your dad's. You know how to brush it, right?*

I was startled by her hand on my hair, by our closeness in that moment. I didn't want it to end, didn't want to say, *Of course I know how to brush my own hair. I've been doing it for twenty-eight years!*

How do I do it? I asked, handing her the brush. She told me to hold the hair in the middle, then start by running the brush through the ends first.

You have to do it in sections, she said. *You don't want to cause breakage.* I told her I never knew that before, although I'd learned it from a YouTube video years ago. I thanked her for showing me, told her I wished she'd been able to show me when I was younger.

Those kinds of moments were rare. Rare enough that that one stands out, like the time she got me a maxi pad in the visiting room. Maybe prison had changed her too much. Maybe I had changed too much. She wasn't how I thought she would be, and maybe she thought the same thing about me. She didn't remember the same things I remembered, like Nick's big soccer games or going on trips with Craig.

Was I there? she'd always ask, or, *Where was I?* I felt like I couldn't recognize her, couldn't find the person I'd known when I was a child. I started to realize that we'd experienced the night of the murder so differently—it was almost like we weren't there together at all. Whenever she talked about the murder, she only talked about Nick and herself, like she didn't even remember me being there.

I thought back to when she and I were alone in my room, waiting for the police to come while Nick was in Betty's room on the phone with the dispatcher. I'd never forgotten that moment when she realized there was blood on her shirt, how she stood up and asked if she was bleeding. I guessed she didn't even remember that, how I tried to calm her down, gave her a glass of water, told her it was all going to be okay.

Mom, I told her one afternoon, it *hurts my feelings when you erase me from that night. I was there.* She looked surprised, taken aback. She wasn't used to me saying things like that, being honest. I felt like I was doing something wrong, like a little kid fessing up to something. I never usually spoke up for myself.

Okay, she said. *Sorry.*

When Nathan was in class or teaching, I'd sit and watch TV with her, just like before she went to prison; it was still her favorite thing to do.

Want to come to yoga class? I'd ask.

Want to walk the dog together?

Want to help me cook?

I don't like doing anything, she'd say. *I just want to lie down.*

So the only way we could spend time together was watching TV or going to Target, which was her other favorite thing.

She loved watching murder mysteries, especially about wrongful convictions. We watched HBO's *The Undoing,* where Hugh Grant is accused of murdering the younger woman with whom he cheated on his wife.

Bludgeoning her to death. We watched *Defending Jacob,* about a high school boy accused of murdering a classmate. Stabbing him to death with a knife that went missing.

This is like what happened to me, Mom would say sometimes, sounding paranoid. *They framed me.* I never knew what to say. I watched these shows with my hands over my face, peeking through my fingers to look at Mom. She never flinched, never looked away.

There's no doubt about this matter being a very bloody affair.

—Defense Attorney, *State v. A.D.*, 2009

The thirteenth anniversary of the murder came three months after Mom was released. We hadn't been together on that day since it happened, and it was impossible not to think of it that way. Every year was different. Every year I felt different. Sometimes I felt excited to remember Betty, and other times, I felt exhausted, depressed. Some years, especially in the beginning, I just wanted to stay in bed. In recent years, I started committing to doing *something* for the anniversary, even if it was something small like eating a piece of chocolate, watching an episode of *Jeopardy!*, or lighting a candle. Most years, Nathan and I made an altar for her, something his family did to honor their dead in Mexico.

I didn't know how to include Mom in this or if I was supposed to include her. Although she and Val didn't have a relationship anymore, she always talked about how Val was the only person who sent her a condolence card when she first got to the county jail. How nobody else bothered to say, *I'm sorry for the loss of your mother*. I wasn't sure if I was supposed to say that now, if I was supposed to make this day about Mom and her loss. When she was in prison, she never called on birthdays or holidays. She certainly never called on the anniversary of the murder. Those days were too difficult, she had told me when I was younger, and they reminded her how alone she was. I somehow felt responsible, like it was my fault she was alone on those important days. It was hard to hold that guilt along with the longing to hear my mother's voice, to be wished a happy birthday by the person who brought me into this world.

Nathan came up with the idea of driving down the coast to 17-Mile Drive to show Mom Pebble Beach. It wasn't a very far drive, just a quick trip down Highway 1. When I first moved to California, I was surprised that May was always one of the coldest months. It was usually foggy and gray, the marine layer hanging over the coastline. But that day was beautiful. Warm enough and surprisingly sunny. Mom wore a fuzzy pink sweater and pink Adidas sneakers she'd gotten at Kohl's when we first brought her home.

We didn't really talk about Betty. I tried to bring up memories like I did with Nathan every year on the anniversary, but Mom wouldn't engage. I'd bring up things I used to do with Betty—going to the bookstore, going to the flea market, listening to tapes in the Jeep. Mom either said she didn't remember that or didn't say anything at all. We got out of the car at each of the lookout points, took pictures in front of the ocean among groups of eager tourists. Mom didn't want to take off her sunglasses for our selfies because she didn't like the way she looked. In one photo, I'm hugging her, smiling, my long, frizzy hair covering her face.

When we got home from our day trip, Nathan and I made an altar of things that represented Betty. I thought we had a good day. I thought we had fun, laughed, and smiled. Enjoyed the fresh air and each other's company. Did something special together for the first time in so long. There were pictures to prove it. Making the altar felt right, like it wouldn't offend Mom or make her upset. On the dining table, we displayed one of my favorite photos of Betty that Mom's cousin had given me. In it, she's young, though I don't know how young, with long hair and a giant dog, cigarette in hand as always.

Right in front of it, we put out three small oranges, a small Lindor dark chocolate ball like the ones I used to eat with her on the couch while we watched our shows. An avocado in honor of the time she made me try guacamole at the taco shop near the casino. A few of Nathan's succulents in colorful little pots, a nod to the collection of cacti she used to keep in the corner of her room.

Who is that? Mom said, pointing to the picture frame. Nathan and I looked at each other, confused.

It's Betty, we said at the same time.

That's not my mom, she replied, taken aback.

Seeing an oncologist, preparing for another surgery outside of prison, was part of Mom's medical parole. Once she got an ID and Medicaid, Nathan and I drove her to her appointments with Dr. Lee to keep up with her scans, ensure that the tumor wasn't growing or spreading. Most of the assistance she got was thanks to Nathan spending hours on the phone, trying to advocate for her. He'd done this at his old job in the Bronx, where he'd helped recently arrived immigrant mothers navigate the confusing world of social services and government programs. He knew how to talk to the annoyed or apathetic operators at call centers, knew how to ask the right questions. After Mom moved in, he'd finish studying for his qualifying exams in the morning, then block out a window of time to get on the phone, try to get Mom some help in the afternoon.

Going to Mom's medical appointments was difficult with the ankle monitor strapped to her leg. Almost everything was more difficult with the ankle monitor: she had to charge it every night by sitting right next to an outlet, it beeped loudly and randomly at the most inconvenient times, it made sleeping and showering uncomfortable for her. Plus, people stared. She asked her parole officer if she could have it removed for her appointments when she needed to get tests or MRIs, and he agreed after some hesitation. He didn't want to drive to our apartment *just* for that every time she had an appointment, so he gave Nathan permission to cut it off at home.

The kitchen scissors were too weak, so he used a box cutter as Mom propped her leg up on the ottoman in the living room. That was one of the only times I saw Mom genuinely smile or let out a real laugh—when she watched the thick black band break away from her skin. She was supposed to wear the ankle monitor for the entirety of her parole—two years—and now she had some amount of freedom back after a matter of months. Nobody tracking her, nothing for the nurses to stare at in doctors' offices.

Soon after the monitor was off, we found out there was no cancer. It was a false alarm. During an appointment with Mom and me, Dr. Lee told us there was no mass, no tumor growing. Just an error on a scan she'd been given by the prison doctor. An optical illusion. Probably just extra tissue. The news was shocking: this was the whole reason she'd gotten out of prison early. Nathan and I asked each other countless questions in whispers in the garage. What did this mean? Was she still *allowed* to be out of prison? Would she have to go back? What were we supposed to do? Should we call someone?

I'd learned—or relearned—that Mom never showed much emotion about anything. She didn't react, hardly ever showed surprise, disappointment, or even happiness.

You train yourself not to feel when you're in here, she'd told me over the years. Now I was finally seeing it for myself. She insisted nobody needed to know about the false diagnosis, not even her parole officer. After all, he never asked questions about her health, only gave her the monthly urine test in our shared bathroom, poked around the kitchen cabinets looking for alcohol, and left.

When we first picked Mom up from prison, I wondered what would happen if the cancer got worse, if she died under our care, in our apartment. While she'd been living with us, while I'd thought the cancer was growing, that fear kept coming up, and I tried to push it away. I couldn't stand the thought of another home tainted by death. The first home I'd felt truly safe in as an adult was the first apartment Nathan and I shared way uptown in Manhattan, and we'd continued building our own version of that safe place in California. We didn't have a lot of money, and most of our furniture was thrifted, but we loved the home we'd made together.

Now that there was no cancer, I thought life might get easier. After her first surgery when she'd gotten the tumor removed, she told me she had *a new lease on life*. Maybe she'd feel that way again. Maybe we'd fall into a rhythm. Maybe Mom would be happy here. But she had other ideas. Now, she told us, she could focus on her back pain, her nerve problems that had developed and then worsened throughout her sentence. Suddenly, we had a new project: getting Mom's back treated. I'd gotten her organic essential oils and every form of Icy Hot to try to numb the pain. I tried to give her CBD ointment, but she feared it would show on her monthly drug tests, so she never used it.

Through Medicaid, she was able to establish care with a well-known spine doctor in the Bay Area whose years of accolades had been the focus of a story in the *New York Times*. Testing determined that Mom's nerves in her lower back had been compressed, practically crushed, from all those years of sitting and sleeping on the metal prison stools and beds. Her new doctor fast-tracked her fusion back surgery that would place a permanent metal cage between her vertebrae. I learned online that back surgery was tricky. For many patients, it either didn't make a difference or made the pain even worse. I was relived she would be working with one of the state's best back doctors.

When it was time for the procedure, I drove her an hour and a half to the university hospital. The pandemic had been raging on for the past year, so family members weren't allowed inside the hospital during appointments. I dropped her off with an attendant and told her to update me whenever possible. When I picked her up a few days later, I had to show my vaccine card to get in. The nurse allowed me into the room while she helped Mom go to the bathroom with the door half-open. I tried to focus on packing up Mom's things, gathering her clothes and shoes in the tote bag I brought.

You ready for this? the nurse asked me after she caught me staring.

Coming home from the hospital after an attendant helped me put Mom into my car, we got stuck in bumper-to-bumper traffic. I had an evening class I couldn't afford to cancel, so I had to send my students an email from the highway that I was going to be late. Mom was mostly out of it, told me not to be so uptight about my schedule.

Everything's going to be fine, she said, looking off toward the coast. When we finally made it back home, I couldn't get Mom out of the car or up the stairs to our second-floor apartment. She could stand upright but couldn't walk on her own. Nathan was teaching his own class, so I ran to our neighbor's apartment, and he came out to help her. He had a side job working with Parkinson's patients at a gym for seniors, so he was used to lifting people from falls. He gently carried her out of the car, then guided her up the stairs. He didn't know anything about Mom's life or what led us to this point, but I was so touched by his kindness that I started crying.

It's no big deal, he said. *What are you crying for?*

After I set Mom up in her bed, took a look at her bandages for the first time, tucked her under the covers, I remembered I was late for class. Quickly, I changed my clothes, ran downstairs. When I got to the bottom of the staircase, I realized I didn't even have my backpack or my phone. I ran back up, then back down, and finally got into the car. Looking at the clock, I pulled out of my parking space as fast as I could before I realized I'd backed right into our neighbor's car.

Oh, come on, I shouted, on the brink of a panic attack. I went back to his front door, told him what happened.

That car is older than you, he said, laughing. *Don't even worry about it. Has anyone ever told you that you need to relax?*

Mom started asking her doctors to give her Klonopin again after her back surgery. She was on post-op painkillers for a while, but she wanted more. In the weeks following the procedure, I changed the bandages on her back, and Nathan helped her get around the apartment every time she wanted to stand. Now that she was recovered and off of the pain meds, she listed a variety of reasons she needed Klonopin, like insomnia, panic attacks, and anxiety. She'd been on it for more than twenty years by the time she went to prison, where she was abruptly forced off it and then experienced a days-long withdrawal period of physical illness. Body aches. Vomiting. Cold sweats. Most doctors were against giving it to her, citing the highly addictive nature of the drug—and her decades of dependency on it.

She'd found a doctor in another state who agreed to work with her remotely to prescribe it to her.

Don't do it, Mom, I pleaded. *That stuff is so bad for you, remember? You don't need it. You're doing good now.*

Yes, I do, she said. *There's nothing for me out here. It helps me.*

I had recently reached out to a local nonprofit that specialized in restorative justice. A mild-mannered woman named Claire met with us on Zoom—Mom, Nathan, and me sitting side by side in the kitchen—to create a safe space for a conversation focused on encouraging Mom to move on from the past and begin her future. I had hoped it would be inspiring and even empowering for Mom, but the meeting didn't go as planned. Right before we started, Mom popped the tiny pill into her mouth, and as the minutes passed, she became more and more disconnected from the conversation.

Why didn't my son come? she asked in a baby-like voice. *Why isn't my son here?*

Well, your daughter and soon-to-be son-in-law are here. They want the best for you, said Claire. *They care about you.* We shifted in our seats.

By then, she had gotten her own car, an off-white convertible Mini Cooper. I'd gone with her to the used car dealer a few hours away, gave her some extra money to close the deal. I took a picture of her standing in front of the car with a big red bow on the hood, like a girl on her sixteenth birthday. We went to IHOP and ate pancakes after, parked our cars right next to each other. It was one of our good days that I thought of fondly. I liked knowing Mom wanted to be independent. She'd take her car to Target or the mall, drive it down the Pacific Coast Highway with plastic sunglasses on her face. In the weeks that followed our restorative justice session, Mom became defensive and standoffish at home. She'd leave for most of the day, driving to places she wouldn't tell us about. Since then, as the apartment became more tense, our relationships—mine and hers, Nathan and hers—had begun to spiral.

One night, after Nathan and Mom got into a particularly ugly argument, she stopped eating meals with us. She brought her food to her room and ate on her bed in front of the TV. She didn't say good morning or goodnight anymore. In the evenings, she'd cry loudly as Nathan and I watched TV or played video games, and in the middle of the night, she'd wander through the halls, walking back and forth, using the microwave, or sometimes talking to herself.

One morning in my classroom, I googled, *Klonopin sleepwalking,* which led me to, *Klonopin suicidal ideations.* I wondered about but didn't dare to type *Klonopin violent behavior.*

It was the first day of a new class, the start of a new semester. Only a few students had arrived, quietly unzipping their backpacks, scrolling on their phones. I was shuffling syllabi, setting up the monitor in the new classroom.

Check out the lockdown button, a student said with a grin. I didn't even know his name yet. He kept looking at the button. Red, shiny, intimidating. In previous years, none of my classrooms ever had a lockdown button, but the building had been remodeled. It was our first semester back in person after the pandemic. I was already feeling anxious, uncertain. I tried to force a half smile under my mask, laugh it off.

He brought it up again. Even before the icebreaker was over, even before the first-day nerves could fade. Before we heard where all twenty-two students grew up, what their majors were, what they hoped to become after college. That was how it started, before I would become consumed by my fear for their safety. Before I reported him, then reported him again, hoping each day they would make it out of that room without ever having to see me press the button.

Every class, he questioned everything I did. He rolled his eyes when I asked questions. He sighed loudly when I tried to make a point.

I never learn anything from you, he shouted. *This class is pointless.* I was used to that kind of thing: Dee had been that way when I first got to Rikers, and even all these years later, she remained among my favorite students I'd ever had. This student was different. He was aggressive toward the others, made fun of their speeches, hounded them with impossible questions when they spoke in class.

Are you sure about that? he'd gesture to the statistics on their slides. *That seems pretty stupid.*

I tried to intervene, asked him to stop. I told him it wasn't appropriate.

Sometimes, the students would stay behind after he left.

You're a really good teacher, they said.

This is my favorite class.

He just has it out for you. Nobody knows why.

By then, I assumed he googled me before the semester even began, read about the murder. Students had done this in the past. Like when I was fresh out of grad school, at my first teaching job, when my student came up to me and said, flat out, *Did your mom really kill someone?* I'd heard the question so many times: when my college roommate googled me, whenever an almost-boyfriend googled me.

But you were just a teen then, they'd say when they felt bad. Most of the time, they didn't use it against me. Even if they saw me as a victim, someone they should feel sorry for, they mostly didn't show it.

Maybe he sees you as an easy target, a friend offered when I told her about him, *because of, you know.*

I started to question myself: had my own trauma, my, *you know,* made me overreact? Even my boss knew about my *situation,* that Mom was living with me, that it hadn't been going well. A student presented a speech about gun violence, told us she was accidentally shot as a child when she and a family member found a gun. Students wiped their eyes. He asked to see her scar, wanted her to prove it in front of everyone. Later, he gave a speech about the recent Alec Baldwin shooting on a film set, shared his knowledge about guns: loading them, cocking them, shooting them. He would never make a mistake like Alec did.

It was an evening class. The courtyard outside was always empty. After we got out, I'd go home to find Mom sitting in the same place I'd left her, watching TV shows about wrongful convictions or mysterious celebrity deaths. I was overwhelmed, feeling trapped every morning and night. Mom and I didn't get along the way I hoped we would, and I'd take my Zoom therapy appointments in the car or my office.

My mom just . . . doesn't like me, I'd say, crying so hard I had to turn my camera off. *Why doesn't she like me?* It was all too much. Nathan and I were newly engaged, working on planning our wedding, knowing it would be the first time Nick would see Mom. I was terrified, a knot in my stomach each time I pictured that moment. When anyone asked Nathan why he waited so long—six years—to propose to me, he told them it was because he wanted my mom to be part of it. Now, that thought made me sad, disappointed. I just wanted *something* in my life to make sense, like teaching used to. Before this student stepped into my classroom.

Who will come to save us? I wondered some nights when I walked to class, the sun setting earlier each night, and eventually before class even began. He always arrived first, watched cartoons, or listened to loud music before the others came in. We lived in faculty housing on campus, one mile from the classroom. I was only sleeping two hours a night, wondering if he followed me, if he brought a gun to class that night, or if he would next week. My doctor put me on anxiety medication, told me to relax.

Kids these days, she said, opening the door to show me out. He started coming to class in a black mask, the kind doctors wore during the plague. After I reported him, nothing changed. I sent more emails, asked for help, *stated the details clearly*. Did everything they tell you to do in those training videos.

He's technically not breaking any rules, the administrator said. *His other professors say he's never done or said anything disruptive.*

This would go on for over six months because, after that semester ended, he was allowed to enroll in another course I taught the following spring. The day I saw his name on my roster, I requested the department remove him from the class, referred to the documentation I filed on the student the previous semester. My request was denied, my anxieties dismissed again. I tried to teach the class as I normally would, tried to focus on the other students who wanted to be there.

He kept lashing out. *Everything we talk about is made up bullshit,* he said. *All these topics are just social constructs. Life is a simulation. We're not really here. No one wants to answer your questions. Accept the silence.*

When I asked the students to submit songs for our class playlist for writing sessions, he sent a metal song from the video game *Doom*. When it came on abruptly in class, between instrumental jazz and Lofi beats, students covered their ears, put on their headphones, asked me privately to turn it off.

It scares me, a student told me. *It gives me anxiety.*

Me too, I thought. But I told her that the playlist represented our *community,* that we should respect and celebrate our differences. He banged his head in the corner.

I came home from class crying almost every night. I felt so helpless, so alone. Mom and Nathan would talk to me about it sometimes, but they didn't understand what I felt.

I'm afraid he's going to kill me, I'd say. *Or the other kids. I can't bear the thought of* another *murder. I swear, I'm not just being paranoid.*

After months of workers' comp therapy sessions, I finally decided to resign from teaching at the university, the thing that once brought me joy and hope. In an email, I wrote to my department chair, *I know you are already familiar with my home situation at this time, and I simply cannot afford any additional stress.* When it was finally over, I still thought of his face behind the plague mask. I thought, too, of the night, the year after the murder, when a classmate at my new high school invited me to a haunted house for Halloween. I thought I could do it, thought I wouldn't be scared. The therapy had been helping. I'd finally been able to sleep with the light off. It was what teens were supposed to do on Halloween.

But I didn't even make it to the house, just the line to get in. A masked monster ran out with a chainsaw, clothes torn and soaked with fake blood. Screams and menacing laughter echoed from inside the house. I ran back to the parking lot alone, hid behind some car, hyperventilating.

Will it always be like this? Will it? I said over and over to no one, trying to catch my breath. *Willitwillitwillit?*

For months, even after I started a new job at another university, I would see him everywhere. Shopping at Target. Bagging groceries at the local market. Walking a dog in my neighborhood. Logically, I knew I was safe. It was like when I used to have lucid dreams, convinced that my apartment was being broken into. It felt so real. I told myself he wasn't here, that he'd never find me. Maybe he never wanted to hurt me. Maybe it was just inside my head.

Will it always be like this? I asked again each time, trying to catch my breath.

My wedding week was the first time Nick and Mom talked in at least a decade. He had stopped answering her calls and letters a few years into her sentence, but she asked me about him every time she called. It was always *what's Nick up to* and *how's Nick doing* and *has Nick said anything about me lately*. By the time our fifteen minutes were up, sometimes I'd never even had a chance to say anything about my life.

She tried to call him once she got out of prison, requested him on Facebook multiple times from multiple accounts. But he wouldn't respond. After the ceremony, when our photographer asked all the family members of the bride and groom to stand up for a group shot, I asked Mom to stand next to me. She'd missed so much: my high school graduation, my prom, my college graduation, my MFA graduation. This was the first time she'd ever seen me dressed up, hopeful, crossing a bridge into a new chapter of my life. I wanted it to be like I'd imagined while she was away. Maybe she'd touch my hand or my cheek. Maybe she'd whisper something special in my ear.

I didn't have a wedding party, didn't have a group of women I'd known all my life standing beside me. Instead, Nick was my best man, and he stood next to me as Nathan and I got married. The night before, after Mom had seen him for the first time, then ran out of my rehearsal dinner crying in front of the whole restaurant, he came into my room at the Airbnb. I had been crying so hard I feared no concealer would be able to make me presentable for the wedding in a few hours.

Why is everything like this? Can't there be one good day? I asked. Nick stayed quiet, put his hand on mine. We sat together for a while, and he wouldn't leave the room until I was ready to go to sleep.

When Mom came to stand next to me during the family photo, she didn't squeeze my hand, didn't even say anything to me. She turned back to look at Nick. It was clear she wanted to talk to him after what happened at the rehearsal dinner.

Smile, said the photographer, but she didn't turn back around.

Instead, she asked, *Nicholas, will you go to lunch with me tomorrow?*

Mom! I said, looking around to see Nathan's family all facing forward with genuine smiles on their faces. *We're taking the photo! You're standing next to the bride!* Dad and Val stood by watching, waiting, smiling at the camera.

All night after the pictures, Mom kept following Nick around. I stayed on the dance floor trying not to get Aperol Spritz on my dress, watching each time she'd follow him around a corner.

A friend came up to me and said, *Wow, she really wants to talk to him. You'd think it was his wedding.* I managed a half-hearted laugh.

The day after the wedding, I sat with Nick and Mom at a table at Panera. He said he would only go to lunch with her if I agreed to go, too. So there I was: I'd been married for less than twenty-four hours, should have been packing swimsuits and sunblock for my honeymoon in Palm Springs. Instead, I sat exhausted on the green vinyl seat of a strip mall Panera Bread.

How have you been doing all these years? Mom asked.

Do you ever think about me?

What would it take for you to talk to me again?

I want to be in your life.

Don't you need your mother?

Nick's answers were curt, monotone. Sometimes he wouldn't look up, meet her eyes with his. He'd rub his thumb into his palm over and over—something I used to watch him do in the middle of the field when he was nervous during his soccer games as a kid. I wondered what she thought he'd say.

I'd tried so many times to get Nick to talk to Mom.

She has a card for you, I'd say. *Can I give her your address?*

She has something she wants to tell you.

She's changed, I swear. She's not the person she used to be.

But he never said yes, never asked any follow-up questions.

When she had cancer, he and I went to a bar while I was visiting Florida for the holidays. We sat on two benches outside, and I tried to plead with him: *Our mother has cancer in prison, and I'm the only person she has outside of that place. It's really bad. I can't do this alone.*

He said no.

When we thought she had cancer the second time, he thought about it. When she told me she *might* have only three months to live, he said his girlfriend wanted him to go visit her.

She says I'll regret it, he told me on FaceTime. But he didn't end up going, and after she got out and started seeing Dr. Lee, Mom ended up fine.

At Panera, things took a turn.

You really think I killed my mother? Mom asked, starting to cry into her chicken sandwich.

I don't think, he said. *I know.*

Suddenly, she started to run toward the exit, tears streaming down her face.

Mom, let me drive you home, I said, chasing after her.

Not gonna happen, she said, and she slammed the door in my face.

Nick and I left the restaurant, finding her car still in the parking lot empty. We sat in the rental car he'd gotten for the wedding, watching, waiting until she came back.

We sat in silence. Did she leave the car? Where did she go?

I felt the sting of acid in my stomach, that same feeling I used to get as a child: *my mother is going to hurt herself.* I thought about that night in college when she told me that Nick had killed Betty, that she was just protecting him. Why did she say that? Still, I'd never asked, never even brought it up again.

Soon she came barreling across the street. She'd gone to a 7-11 to buy a pack of cigarettes, though she hadn't smoked since before she went to prison. Instead of getting in the car, she sat down on the curb, rocking back and forth, and lit the cigarette, wailing. A mother and daughter walked by on their way to Panera, looking concerned. The mother shook her head and they continued walking. More people passed by, looking curiously at the woman crouched down crying out loud. Maybe they were wondering: does she know how loudly she's crying? Nick and I just watched.

I almost thought of the murder—of him and me watching her from the back of two police cars, but I told myself: don't do that now. Not again. Not here.

Should we go? I asked. I felt uncomfortable, almost embarrassed.

Let's just see, he said. We stayed like that for some time before Nick put the car in reverse and backed out of the parking lot.

Four days after the wedding, Mom posted on an online forum asking strangers to help her kill herself in our garage. Nathan and I were on our honeymoon in Palm Springs, trying to escape 118-degree weather, waist-deep in the bright blue pool taking tequila shots. We ordered smoked salmon and avocado toast, watched drops of hot sauce float on the surface of the water, and I tried not to think of Mom. I tried not to think of how she looked when I'd last seen her, crying on the curb with a cigarette hanging from her lips.

We hadn't spoken since Panera. One night, while Nathan and I were drinking wine in our Airbnb, she commented *Beautiful!* on my Instagram post about the wedding.

Will a 2009 car running in the garage kill you? she wrote on the forum.

She got a handful of responses.

Any car, any year, any make, or model if it has a gasoline engine running in a garage will kill you. If you don't believe me try it sometime.

Yep. Good news is it'll take a lot longer than a 1979 car.

Inside the garage with no ventilation?? It may or may not, depending on the exposure and the length of time, carbon monoxide will poison your blood!! You may not notice the damage immediately, it could take months or even years!! So stay safe and away from running vehicles in enclosed places!!

It could if the windows and doors are shut tight. With the motor running the car produces carbon monoxide gas which is poison to your lungs.

Are you in there with it? If not. . . . No it will not.

When we got home from Palm Springs, sunburned and hungover, she didn't mention it. I'd soon find out her parole office had threatened to 5150 her for concerning behavior.

We've got to go, I told Nathan one night. We'd started taking our food to go in the evenings, eating on a bench in the dog park or a parking lot. *We can't stay here anymore.*

I couldn't sleep through the night anymore. Not since I'd gotten the call from the officer. Unlike all the police officers I'd talked to on the night of the murder, when they walked in and out of the house with their flashlights and guns, this officer seemed to feel bad about what he had to tell me.

It was a suicide attempt, he said. Someone was walking his dog near the house I'd rented for Mom and found her unconscious in her car.

I thought she was dead, the man would later say. *Or at least in a coma.*

It was the day before her parole would officially end. The day before she would be free. Two years to the day that Nathan and I had picked her up in the prison parking lot. The police officer told me she'd left a note in the passenger's seat. It said *CALL MY DAUGHTER* with my phone number written on it. By the time he called me, she was already in the ambulance on the way to the ER to be treated for carbon monoxide poisoning.

I was on a work call when the police officer told me about the attempt. That night and the following day, I called the hospital over and over, trying to find out if my mom was going to live.

She asked us not to disclose any further information to her daughter, said the nurse.

Most nights, I tried not to wake Nathan up, but sometimes, I couldn't help it. There were nights I felt the walls of our bedroom shrinking around me, the floral-patterned pillows suffocating me. It was like the days, weeks, months after the murder. How I'd see things. How I'd fear closing my eyes. Every night after the attempt, I'd have visions of my mother dying. Or chasing me. I kept wondering what she looked like the day she tried to die. Did she really put on a full face of makeup before she got in the car? I wondered, too, about her method. Her car. The car she'd fought so hard to get after she got out of prison. The only thing she actually owned. The only thing that belonged to her.

Again, I found myself requesting the police report, scouring for details that would make it make sense. There was no mention of how she looked, only how she'd taped a hose to her tailpipe, fed it through the driver's side window, and inhaled exhaust until she lost consciousness. Those nights, Nathan would hold me for a while as I cried into my pillow. I thought of chasing melatonin with NyQuil like I used to, wondered how much it would take not to wake up in the morning.

I joined a virtual support group for family members of people with mental illness and addiction. I tried to explain it all in under two minutes, each participant's allotted time, without crying.

She tried to kill herself in the driveway of the house I'd rented for her under my name and left my phone number on the seat. How much more can I forgive? I asked the thirty tiny square faces staring back at me. *How much more?*

No one responded, so the facilitator moved on to the next person. I sunk down into my chair, turned my camera off. I guess I sound cold-hearted, I thought. They must think I'm a terrible daughter, like the ER nurse did. They probably think, *She should show her mother a little mercy.*

By the end of the night, three other people would describe their family members' suicide attempts, the terror they felt when it happened. The guilt. The responsibility. The fear—mostly the fear. How, eventually, they had to stop *killing themselves* to try to save the other person.

A month after the attempt, my new therapist gave me a list of exercises for insomnia.

If you can't sleep after twenty minutes, stop trying. Get out of bed.

I decided to get up, walked around the living room and looked for a long time at the framed photo on the wall.

It was one of our favorites from our engagement photoshoot the previous year. Nathan and I stand smiling in the sand at Big Sur, a bit of sweat glistening on our faces after our hike down a steep trail among the blooming white lilies. I'm wearing a flower crown I made from supplies I bought at Dollar Tree, and he's wearing a pink suit that fits a little too loose around his legs. In the background, the bluest water you've ever seen: rough and intimidating, dotted with glitter.

We thought splurging on a photographer was both embarrassing and indulgent before we got engaged, but a few months into wedding planning, we booked one. After hours of researching and interviewing photographers, we found Tom, a local high school teacher turned wedding photographer. The night before our engagement photoshoot, we woke to the sound of knocking on the front door. I looked at my phone and saw that Mom had been texting me all night, asking me to come out of my room.

When I answered the door, two police officers stood on the patio, asking me if anyone in the residence was suicidal. Mom had been on the phone with a suicide hotline, one of them said, and the person on the other end sent them to check on her.

Do you believe your mother is going to hurt herself?

Has she ever threatened to hurt herself before?

Are you concerned for her well-being?

I already learned on the bad night how you were supposed to answer police officers' questions.

No, I said.

Not that I know of, I said.

No, I said again.

Thank you very much for coming by, I said, smiling through my night retainer. *And hey, haven't our dogs played together at the dog park before?*

Well, have a good night then, said the officer, and he and his partner turned and left. A few hours later, when it was time to get ready for our photoshoot, Nathan and I stood puffy-faced and swollen-eyed in the mirror. I just hoped I could stop crying before we met Tom at Big Sur.

In the living room, I thought, I don't want to look at this photo and think of my mother wanting to die for the rest of my life. When I was trying to fall asleep, I could have sworn I heard her speaking to me.

You have to call me, she said. *You have to talk to me.*

But I'm not ready, I said just then, to the photograph of Nathan and me. *What if I don't want to?*

The next day, I asked my therapist if I should write a letter to Mom.

I've never not talked to her, I said. *Maybe I should explain myself.*

After she was transferred from the ER to a psych ward, she started calling me every day, sometimes twice a day, despite what the nurse had told me before. She left me voicemails, each time sounding like a different person than she did in the last.

Sometimes she was angry, said she couldn't believe I wouldn't pick up. *Do you even give a fuck about me?* she yelled into the receiver, pissed off. Other times, she wanted to know how I was doing, if I was okay.

I love hearing your voice on your answering machine, she said, sounding like a little girl.

It made me think of when she was in prison, how, even if I couldn't take her call because I was at school or work, I'd still pick up, just to hear the part of the automated recording where she said her name. When I'd slide the button on my phone to answer, the robotic voice would start, *This is a call from,* and then Mom would say her name before the robot would continue, *at a state correctional facility. Press one to answer. Press seven to decline all future calls.* Sometimes I just wanted to hear her voice.

My therapist wanted me to write a letter to myself instead. She said I needed to stop centering my mom and try to center myself.

I like that idea, I told her, smiling. *I'm going to start tonight.*

For two days, I tried to start. *Should I write Dear Self, or should I write out my own name?* I wondered. I stared at the blank document, getting nothing done, and closed my laptop. The next night, I tried again. I ran my fingers through my hair, took a deep breath. I wrote the date in the top right corner because that seemed important, so I could remember the first time I *centered* myself. The words wouldn't come out. I had so much to say but couldn't say it, even here, alone.

I pulled out my phone and typed in: *how to cut your split ends.* I got up, walked to the bathroom, and took out a pair of scissors.

I followed the woman in the video. I tied my hair up into two ponytails and cut in a straight line. I thought of all the things I couldn't say to myself on paper. That it was okay to stop answering. That it was okay to need space. That it was okay, this time, to choose myself. That every night wasn't *the* night. That the fear wasn't going to kill me. That two things could be true: I could be relieved that my mom wasn't dead and also that she was not a part of my life anymore.

This is just to clean up the ends, the woman in the video instructed. *I'm not a professional. Make sure you don't cut too much.* But I kept chopping, until I looked down and saw four inches of my hair on the ground, coarse and golden like a haystack.

Mom didn't wear a lot of makeup when she first got out of prison. She had been overwhelmed by the choices at the stores, signs that said things like *As Seen on TikTok*. She was more worried about her hair, so I found a salon near our apartment and took her to get a haircut and color. When the hairdresser asked how long it had been, I watched Mom watch herself in the mirror as she said, *A long time. At least a decade.* The hairdresser wanted to know why she waited so long, what made her want to change her hair now. Mom's eyes darted, and we quickly changed the subject. I realized soon after we entered this new reality that these moments would happen often. Mom had to hide her ankle monitor from the eyes of strangers, had to deflect certain questions so nobody would find out where she'd been.

My mom got sick so she's living with me for a while, was the story I'd tell people, like the neighbor who'd helped her up the stairs after her surgery. They had so many questions. *What's she sick with? Is it serious? You hadn't mentioned your mom much before. Wait, I thought you had a brother. Why doesn't he take her in?*

Soon, I got better at making up stories, coming up with my own methods of deflecting. After all, I'd always had to do that. When she went on trial. When she got sentenced. When I got mail and phone calls from the prison. When she was absent for half my life. I always had to have some reason, always had to satiate the curiosities of others.

One of the only remaining baby pictures of me is of Mom holding me. I don't recognize the background, but it must be one of our early houses from before. Before there were all these secrets, before we moved so many times, before we fell apart. Maybe Dad even took the photo. In it, Mom has warm blonde, choppy hair with bangs and she wears a very '90s denim dress. I'm just a tiny blob wearing a white dress and a white headband. What I loved most about the picture the first time I saw it were her nails. They're long and red and almond shaped, maybe even done professionally at a salon. While she was away, I framed the picture and placed it on a table in my living room, somewhere I'd see it every day.

When she got out, I gestured to the picture on the end table, which was now next to what would become her spot on the couch.

Those nails, she said. *I want to wear them like that again.* She looked closer at the picture. *I don't remember that day at all.*

I'd desperately wanted to paint my nails that color, too. I'd collected reds over the years but none of them matched. The red she wore in the photo wasn't bright, but it wasn't dark. The disposable camera photo was grainy, so it was hard to tell whether the polish was matte or had a kind of sheen to it.

Within a few months, Mom started wearing makeup again. Spraying floral perfumes and mists into the air. Washing her hair with fragranced shampoos and conditioners that lingered after she showered. Doing her nails with my box of nail supplies in her bedroom. I always imagined she'd be impressed by my collection. I'd been obsessed with painting my nails since she went away, and whenever I was triggered or upset, I picked the polish off in tiny strips. I knew she couldn't do her own nails in prison, so I started doing mine. In college, my collection grew as I saved Pinterest boards of polka dot nail designs and DIY marbling techniques. I posted my own designs in the early days of Instagram, photos oversaturated with filters and effects. I had glitter and dotting tools and cuticle remover and painters' tape to create lines and color blocks.

I was happy that Mom had started looking like herself again, though it was strange to think my own mother wasn't *herself* without a full face of makeup on. Seeing her like that, all made up, reminded me of times with her I'd forgotten. I thought of one day in the fourth grade when she did my makeup like hers in her bathroom. I sat on the counter while she dusted my cheeks, blended dark powder onto my eyelids.

I look like you! I said, watching her in the mirror when she was done. But when Craig came home, he got mad.

She doesn't need to wear all that, he scolded her. *Let her be a kid.* I went to my room.

Seeing Mom every day again made me feel nostalgic for a time I couldn't remember. Maybe a time that never even existed. I was determined to find that red nail polish from my baby photo, or at least something close enough, and ask Mom if we could paint our nails together. I'd thought of doing that for so long. Months had passed since we'd first talked about it, but I always looked for that shade. One afternoon, I was at the beauty supply store when I finally saw what I thought could be the exact polish I'd been looking for. It was in an OPI bottle labeled *An Affair in Red Square.*

I've been looking for this everywhere, I told the cashier, who couldn't have been more uninterested. *I can't wait to show my mom. She used to wear this color when I was a baby.*

When I got home, I took the small bottle out of the bag and presented it to Mom, who was scrolling on the laptop I'd given her when she got out. She loved online shopping, looking for clothes she used to own before she went away.

It's An Affair, I started.

In Red Square, she finished. *Yeah, I remember that one.*

I was surprised she knew the name. She'd never mentioned it when we talked about the old photo of us—how her nails stood out more than anything.

Isn't it great? I asked, eager to sit down and paint our nails together.

You know, I never liked wearing red, she said. *It doesn't look good on my skin.* She went to her room to take a nap.

When I told her I was moving after the wedding, that she wasn't invited to come with Nathan and me, I told her to take the nail polish she wanted from the box that was once mine but became ours. One of the only things we truly ever shared.

You can take whatever you want, I told her. *Even if it was here before you moved in.*

After I unpacked in my new home, I found the box of nail polish and saw that she'd taken some of my things as I'd recommended, but she left that red polish.

An Affair in Red Square, I said to no one as I broke down another cardboard box.

The Reddit threads and TikTok videos called it *going no contact.* I'd become obsessed with reading and listening to other people's stories about so-called mommy issues, emotionally immature parents, parenting one's own parent. I watched internet therapists act out scenarios between mothers and daughters and saw myself in them. In one, they even showed a mother buying her daughter gifts and then taking them away soon after while the child was at school. They talked about the mother wound, a term for what they called *psychological scars* caused by a mother not meeting their child's needs in early life. The creators of these videos said things like, *It's okay that your mother doesn't like you.* Or, *Do you have a toxic mom who triggers you? Here's how to heal!* The more humorous takes said things like, *Don't fuck with a bitch whose mother was her first hater!*

I decided to block Mom's phone number the night she got out of the psych ward. We hadn't spoken in over a month, since before she tried to kill herself. Since then, her parole had officially ended. Her birthday had passed. It felt impossible not to reach out to her, to tell her I loved her. I wanted to wish her a happy birthday, congratulate her on being a free woman. These were the things I'd thought about while she was gone: celebrating together, like mothers and daughters do. Sharing things, good things.

When she called, I couldn't bring myself to pick up. I didn't know what to say. I wasn't sure if I was sorry for anything, and that made me feel like a bad person. A bad daughter. When she got her cell phone back, the first thing she did was call me, leave a voicemail like she had while she'd been in treatment.

I was unconscious for fifty-nine hours, and you can't even call me back? What the fuck is wrong with you? As soon as the *click* came, I dropped my phone on the floor and immediately threw up. I couldn't control myself. I was sweating and shivering like I had a hangover or the flu, hot and cold at the same time. I felt like a baby, some inconsolable child. I sat doubled over on the bathroom tile, sobbing as I had when I'd gotten the call from the police officer who said, *It was a suicide attempt.*

I feel like I've been nauseous for years, I told Nathan as he sat with me, running his hand through my sweaty hair. *But nothing ever came up. I could never get it out.*

For weeks, I kept going back to one voicemail she'd left me just over two weeks after the attempt.

Maybe someday we'll talk again. Who knows. I've been here seventeen days. I wanted you to know that I decided that I was never going to have another birthday alone. And then I did have one. So that's why I did what I did. That was my decision. That was my main reason. I was like, how can I live without my children? I can't. It's really, really, really, really hard. It's too large to even explain. So I probably won't call you anymore. I love you very much.

The weekend of our first wedding anniversary, Nathan and I drove to New Mexico for the first time since we'd picked Mom up. I thought of riding in the passenger's seat toward the prison, watching the trees and cacti and mountains, thinking the hard part was over, thinking the loss was over. It hurt to think of the possibility of that moment. How we could have started a new life together, how we could have changed the way things had always been. Remembering the anticipation now, I had to stop myself from crying. By the time we decided to take the anniversary trip, I hadn't spoken to Mom in almost six months.

At first, each day felt impossible. I had picked up my old habit of skin picking: digging my nails into the skin of my shoulders and thighs, scratching until blood pooled. Nathan had been upset when he discovered I'd been doing this. He was scared, disappointed.

Why do you want to hurt yourself? he asked. Nobody had ever asked me that before. It gave me some kind of release, something to do with myself as I constantly thought of calling her, apologizing. Telling her I missed her. Offering to help her, promising to save her. But I never did. Each time, I put the phone back down, closed the email draft, made myself bleed.

It was around this time I started saying, definitively, *Mom killed Betty* for the first time. Fifteen years had passed. I was thirty now. It was time to face it, stop living in a *fantasy world,* as my old therapist from when I was sixteen used to say. There was nothing I could do to change the past, to undo anything that had happened. I thought of all the times I told Mom I knew it wasn't her, that someone must have broken in. Did I ever really believe that? Or was I just so afraid of losing Mom that I lied? Who was I trying to protect? She was already gone, already convicted.

I want to see it, I told Nathan after I looked up my old house on Google Maps. *I just want to see what it looks like now.* Years before, I couldn't stomach the sight of my old house. Seeing photos of the house, the turquoise door Betty had picked out made me physically ill. Now that I was trying to put this behind me, finally accept the truth of what happened, I felt a need to go back there.

We'd gotten a trendy Airbnb in Taos, far enough away from my old town for me to feel safe but close enough to stop by and look. We still wanted to celebrate our anniversary, get out of our routines, and spend time together. We'd stocked up on wine at Trader Joe's, brought a bundle of firewood for the outdoor fireplace on the patio. We packed the top layer of our wedding cake in a cooler in the backseat. It had become painful to think of our wedding because it had come to represent one of those moments that changed everything. I'd been working through my experience at Panera with Nick and Mom in therapy, started to recognize it as the rift that could never be repaired.

When we got to town, we started with the supermarket where Nick used to work. Walking through the aisles, it felt like the whole store was still frozen in 2008, like I'd see my brother or one of his friends mopping the aisles in a Hollister polo, piercings sticking out of their noses and lips. But I didn't recognize anyone, and they didn't recognize me. Across from the supermarket in the same plaza was the old building that used to be the video store where Mom worked for a while. I looked in the window and could almost see my fourteen-year-old self, sitting on the counter, deciding which movie I'd play on the big TVs above the shelves of DVDs. *Legally Blonde* if I didn't want Mom to say anything and make me change it, *Hard Candy* if I was feeling edgy. In the back was the creepy room that once housed the porn behind an old beaded curtain. I'd snuck in once when Mom was outside smoking a cigarette, then ran out with my face and ears burning from embarrassment.

Further down the road was the casino, the parking lot emptier than it used to be. The hotel where Nick and I slept after the murder was still there, though it had been eclipsed by a fancy new Hilton hotel a few miles away. I walked into the casino sure I'd run into one of Mom's old boyfriends, or maybe some boy I used to know who'd become one of those men, the kind who sit at the slot machines ordering from the drink cart in the middle of the day. I wondered if anyone from my old high school worked there, if I'd see anyone I knew. I looked around, anxious, uncomfortable, like I was never supposed to come back here. It didn't have the same magic it used to: the one-armed slot machines Betty used to play had been replaced by digital ones with touchscreens and emojis. Everything felt smaller than it had back then, as if I could see the whole place from one spot.

I walked back toward the poker room where Betty worked. There was still the small ramp that led up to it, where I'd sneak up on Betty at the poker table, give her the signal that I was out of school, ready to head home when she was. The physical room was still there, but the tables were gone, as was the sign that read *Poker Room*. I couldn't bring myself to walk in, afraid that it would hurt too much, make all of this real again. After the murder, Betty's boss had hung up a plaque that had her name and photo on it, a gesture that always stayed with me, made me feel like she wouldn't be forgotten.

All these years, I'd imagined that photo still hanging on the wall in the poker room, even if the staff that knew her had come and gone. I imagined it letting strangers know she'd been here once, that she mattered. But it was gone now, all of the walls lined with slot machines instead. The center of the room where I could picture her dealing cards was filled with a row of them. *Pirate's Treasure! Buffalo Link! Grand Jackpot!* There was no sign of Betty, no sign of the life she'd lived here.

Excuse me, I asked a young woman pushing a drink cart down one aisle, a job Mom had for a few weeks one year. *When did they close the poker room?*

We had a poker room? she asked, raising an eyebrow.

When we got back on the road to the old house, I recognized so much and so little at once. I pointed out old classmates' houses and other places I used to know. I saw my old bus stop up the road from one of our old-old houses, where I used to wait each morning and listen to my first-ever iPod, the pink one Betty bought me in middle school that I filled with illegally downloaded emo songs. But there were new things, too, new places I'd never get to know. When we got to the neighborhood, even the street where the house was, the trip started feeling eerie, uncomfortable. I felt scared, like something bad was going to happen.

We pulled into the driveway, which no longer had the circle of lights Nick had installed. The once turquoise door had been replaced, its four matching pillars repainted a dark brown. There were Christmas lights up even though it was August. The weeds were overgrown, a hose snaking out along the unkempt gravel where I'd watched Mom run off into the black night in her bloodstained shirt. Two white cars sat in the driveway, parked in different directions than Betty, Mom, and Nick used to park theirs.

That's not where they're supposed to park, I tried to say, but I couldn't. The cars were blocking the windows to Betty's room, the place where she'd cried for help, where the court said she fought for her life.

She was a fighter, the prosecutor had said.

I can't do this, I told Nathan. *We have to go. Now.*

The sight was sickening, disorienting. I thought of the first day after the murder, when the newspaper printed a photo of the house behind the yellow caution tape. *SCENE OF SUSPECTED MATRICIDE,* the headline read. I remembered my name was spelled wrong in one of the first articles that came out. They said a teen girl named Christy was there, hiding while her grandmother died. They said police confirmed she was not a suspect in the crime. Another article got my age wrong, said the girl in the bedroom was sixteen, not fifteen. Part of me wondered if it was better when the bloody mattress still stood outside that first time I came back to see, when the house was vacant. At least it meant this was Betty's house. At least it proved this was where it all happened. Looking at it now, like this, was like watching a movie someone else made about my life, but almost everything on the screen was false, impossibly wrong.

As we pulled away after the drive that took far longer than the few minutes we actually spent there, I wondered if they—the new owners or tenants, whoever they were—knew what happened in that room. When I finally pulled myself together a few miles down the road, I sat up in the passenger's seat. I pulled out my phone and searched for a song, tried to sing along through tears once the sound came through the speaker: *I will remember you. Will you remember me?*

When I decided to return to New Mexico, I submitted my final request for records to the local police department. I had sent requests over the years, gathering bits and pieces as more questions came to me. I wondered what ever happened to the pajamas and shoes I was wearing that night that had been taken in as evidence. I still wonder if the police officers who watched me undress ever thought of me, if they even remembered me. When I asked to see the videos of our interrogations, a staff member at the police department told me that no such videos ever existed, although tapes were played at Mom's trial in 2009. When I asked to see transcripts of my interviews with detectives, every single one was redacted, entire pages blacked out. *Per NMSA Chapter 32A Children's Code 32A-4-33, as you were a minor at the time of the incident,* said the clerk who gave me the files.

An interview was conducted with [redacted]. She is fifteen years old. She stated [redacted]. She stated [redacted]. She stated [redacted]. She stated [redacted] stated [redacted] When asked [redacted] stated [redacted]. She stated [redacted]. She stated [redacted] stated [redacted]

Excerpt of my redacted police interviews.

I then made contact with Nick, age 18. Nick stated that he was asleep in his room when he heard what he described as a "howl." He stated he had never heard that kind of noise before. He stated he got out of bed but did not immediately run out. His sister then came banging at his bedroom saying "something happened to Betty." He then went to Betty's bedroom [where he saw her] with blood all over herself. He stated he went over to where his grandmother was and checked her vital signs, she had none. He stated he touched her on the back and she was still warm. He stated she was face down in a pool of blood and believed [he saw] what he thought [was] vomit on her. He stated he knew she was dead by the way she felt and looked.

At the Sheriff's Department I conducted an interview with A.D. [She] was read her Miranda Warnings and signed a waiver. A.D. began by saying she knew she was going to jail. She was saying because of "what happened to my mother." She told me that if I was looking for a knife it would be in the dishwasher. A.D. was evasive when answering questions, her answers were irrelevant and [she] would say she didn't remember what occurred. She came out and said if I was looking for a knife there was one in the dishwasher. She stated it might have blood on it because of a cut she got the night before making dinner. She had no visible injuries to her hands and later denied making the statement. While I was looking at A.D.'s hands she told me I wasn't going to find any blood because she had cleaned up prior to police arrival.

—Santa Fe County Sheriff's Department Offense Report,
May 14, 2008

I only have one photo of Betty and me. I'll never know if any others existed before our life was broken open, before hers was taken away. She died just before smartphones took over, before we all started walking around with cameras in our pockets, documenting every moment of our lives. In 2008, I had a green LG camera phone with limited storage, maybe just some selfies or pictures of the dogs. I hadn't taken any pictures of her on it, hadn't considered the importance of remembering her face through a picture on a screen.

There had been a few photo albums in the house, stored somewhere in a plastic bin. Some of our belongings were stolen after someone broke in, but I never wanted to know which ones had been taken or why. Sometimes I'd imagine what it must have looked like in there after everything was packed up, taken away, even the mattress. I wondered if, when the person walked in to take what they could find and go, the cigarette smoke still lingered.

A janitor from the high school had come to the house after the investigation was over to clean up the crime scene. That's something you don't learn from the movies: the family has to make their own arrangements to clean up the blood after everything is photographed and logged and filed. By then, Mom was gone already, in the county jail where she would await her trial for another year. I wondered if she did any sort of act of remembrance for Betty, a makeshift memorial in the confines of her cell.

There is no place for me to go to grieve Betty. None of the photos I have of her are photos that I took, most of them don't represent any of the memories we shared together. I can't remember where exactly we went to scatter her ashes, wouldn't even be able to point it out on a map if I tried. I probably won't try to visit the house ever again. Over time, I trained myself not to bring her up or say her name because I know it just reminds people of what happened to her, how brutal it was. It makes them too uncomfortable, makes them think about the evil in the world. How people can kill. How people get killed.

At home with Nathan, we talk about her. We look at those photos of photos printed out on our bookshelf, and we talk about the places on my face that look like hers, especially as I get older. We both say her name, and I tell him stories about her. Some nights we lie in bed and imagine what it'd be like to have our own daughter—how we'd like to name her Betty and how every time we'd say it out loud, we'd celebrate the life she lived. It wouldn't mean forgetting how she died because that would be impossible.

Nathan helps me remember the good parts, the parts when she was alive. He doesn't ask me to go back, to revisit the hard things, like everyone else always did. I think of things like how whenever I'd accidentally let a bad word slip, in the heat of an argument, she'd say, *Hey, Kris, don't you start fuckin' cursing! It's the worst goddamn habit.* Or how she'd make me a BLT some nights when it was just us two.

There are some things about her that I can't remember anymore, like her laugh. I know she had a raspy voice, almost as if she'd started to go hoarse from all the smoking. But her laugh has gone missing. I think it's been replaced by the screaming from that night, how she sounded when she kept telling us all that she was burning. I try not to think too much about that because it's the kind of detail that can never make sense, never be okay. I try not to, but I still catch myself wondering. Maybe she thought she was on fire. Maybe that was the only explanation for the pain she was in, how fast it was all happening. But I don't know if that's true. I don't have any answers. Maybe I misheard what she said altogether and all the records of me saying that are false. All the times someone asked me to repeat that, the part about the burning, to speak up a little louder, maybe it was the wrong word all along. Maybe she said something else entirely.

There are questions I still want to ask but know that I never will because I know there will be no right answers, just as there have never been any right answers. There is nowhere to turn, no place to mourn, nothing left to investigate. There is only memory, and that's not enough to tell me why, to teach me anything new. Even now, there are days when I wake up and ask myself if all of this really happened. It feels impossible to come to terms with something so violent, like I'm just stuck in an endless movie about a murder and I can't turn it off.

In the closing arguments of the trial, after five days of testimonies and photos from the scene and recordings from all of our interrogations, Mom's lawyer turned to the jury and said, *Ladies and Gentlemen, thank God I'm finished. I won't bore you any longer, although I don't know how you can be bored on this one, because this is definitely one that keeps you on the edge of your seat.*

From the beginning, it seemed that nobody could talk about Betty's death without the language of movies and TV, of entertainment. Now, I realize, there's no way for me to talk about what I've lost without that language either. I don't have the gift of Betty's laughter stored away someplace in my memory, but I still have those nights when we'd be detectives of our own, obsessed with cracking made-up cases we'd forget about in a week. The things that remind me most of Betty, that bring me closest to her, are the sounds and images of violence, of murder.

When I think of our trips to the bookstore, where she saw me in ways no other adults ever had before, I can only picture her in the mystery section. She was just a woman who liked murder mysteries—melodramatic page-turners that kept her guessing until the truth was finally revealed—never knowing that at the end of her life, her legacy would be clouded by one just like those she read about every night before bed. Still, I like to think of her standing there in the aisle, wearing one of her vests with a pile of James Patterson and John Grisham thrillers in her arms, deciding which murder story she'd like to take home this time. When we got home, she'd add the new hardcover to the stack of books beside her bed where the whole thing happened one night.

The last time I saw my mother was the day I moved out of California. I'd resigned from teaching after the incident with the student, so we couldn't live in our on-campus apartment anymore. In my new house, I still looked at her blog, the forum where she'd sought advice about killing herself in the garage. I read her replies to other formerly incarcerated people hoping to write books about their experiences, share their stories with the world.

Can someone help me write my book? I'm incarcerated and have a testimony and life story to tell, wrote one user in a forum about life after prison.

Meeeeee tooooooooooo! Mom responded. I could always tell when she'd logged on after taking her pills. *Please help me. I have a mind-blowing true crime story. But you can't profit from your own crime.*

I started a burner account to look at her profile on Facebook, looked at pictures she uploaded of herself showing bangs she'd obviously cut by herself, a series of new piercings lining her entire ear from top to bottom. She never smiled in the photos.

My ink, she captioned one photo, showing off a tattoo she'd gotten, though she always swore she hated tattoos. When I got a tattoo in college, she told me she hated it.

That's what prisoners do, she said in the visiting room during our trailer visit. *Lowlifes. Trashy people. Why would you want to scar your body forever?*

In the photo, her tattoo looked like it was on her leg, maybe her shin. It was the face of a blonde woman wearing full makeup with a cigarette hanging out of one side of her lips. BORN TO KILL, it said on the helmet she was wearing. It was a female version of the character Joker from Stanley Kubrick's Vietnam War film *Full Metal Jacket.* I never even knew she liked that movie.

It looks like me, Mom continued in the photo's caption.

When we lived in the on-campus apartment, we had a smart garage door opener that connected to our phones, notified us when one of us accidentally left it open. Even though it doesn't work anymore, I still keep the app on my phone now. It tells me how many days it's been closed, how many days since we packed the place up, stood in the driveway and left that part of our lives behind. I always think of how Mom wanted to kill herself there, in the garage where I stored all her crochet projects, her dolls and hats.

I can't control the garage from my phone anymore, but I still open the app to see how many days have passed since then. At first, I was shocked by thirty. Then I was shocked by fifty. It stung to reach over one hundred. Now it's been almost a thousand days since I saw her. Since I touched her. Since I smelled her hair, looked into her eyes. Said I loved her to her face even though it would never be enough.

She lives somewhere in an RV, documents her life on a website under a different name. She posts about having cancer again, says she has a 13 percent chance of survival.

My daughter abandoned me, she writes. *I'm homeless with cancer. Will you please donate to my GoFundMe?*

I think of donating anonymously, giving her all my money. I think of calling her, wonder what she might say if I did. I still listen to her voicemails I saved on my phone, even the cruel ones that break my heart. I want to hear her voice, want to tell her I care. That it matters to me if she suffers. That it matters to me if she dies. That I will be different if she's not on this planet anymore. These wants make no sense to the other people I love. I know she won't, can't care for me back. I know it's pointless to imagine she might someday. I spent almost thirteen years doing that while she was gone and learned the truth the hard way.

What would I even say when she answered?

Hi Mom, am I in trouble?

Hi Mom, are you mad at me?

I refresh her Facebook page over and over again almost every day, look for updates. I ask Nathan to block the page on my phone, make it so I stop obsessing over her, staring at her photos. It works for a few months, but then, I start again: making a new email address to search her name in the middle of the night, scrolling through all her posts as Nathan sleeps beside me. I zoom in on her selfies, pinching my phone screen to try to recognize the person pictured. I save everything in a file on my computer, screenshots of a woman I no longer know. *Is this really my mother?* I ask sometimes, like I did when I sat down to testify at sixteen, mesmerized by her long hair. I know I can't call her. I can't put any ideas in her head that we might be together again someday, can't even tell her I love her.

Instead, I paint my nails that shade of red I'd chased for so long. I gloss my lips mauve, dust the apples of my cheeks pink, apply mascara the way she taught me. I button my jeans, straighten my shirt. Wear a pair of shoes she wouldn't like. My hair is as frizzy as ever, but I'm still waiting for my first gray to come. As I get older, I look in the mirror and I see my mother and my grandmother. I see the same lines around my mouth, the shape of their chins and jaws. My one tooth sticks out like Mom's, my eyes are green like Betty's. When I see myself in the mirror, I can't tell if my face has actually changed or if I'm just looking for signs of them. Proof that they existed. That they were part of me. That they made me.

Sometimes, I imagine taking one last ride in the Jeep, the age I am now, my hair blowing out the open window, heading to that old bookstore that no longer exists. She lights up a smoke with the car's cigarette lighter, holds the rest of the pack up, as if to offer me one now that I'm old enough. I shake my head, tell her that's one habit of hers I never picked up. The swearing, though, that's a different story. She tilts her head back and laughs, and it's like hearing my favorite song from childhood twenty years later, remembering every lyric by heart. There it is, that sound.

Hey, Kris, she says, *How about when we get home, we watch one of our shows? I'll bet I can guess who did it.*

The only known photo of Betty and me, taken approximately 2002.

Nick and Betty sometime in the early '90s.

ACKNOWLEDGMENTS

First, I would be remiss not to acknowledge the very real people mentioned in this book, however briefly, that I never met but whose lives were taken or forever changed by violence: Carlie Brucia, Janet Frake, Sonja Larson, Christina Powell, Christa Hoyt, Tracy Paules, Manuel Taboada, Nicole Brown Simpson, Ron Goldman, Hae Min Lee, and the Alday family. Their legacies are more than what happened to them. Let's continue to say their names.

There were many times over the past decade that I thought I'd never finish this book. I have so many people to thank for making it possible. I am endlessly thankful to Sarah Shermyen, Nicole Walker, Beth Snead, and the team at UGA Press for seeing something in this project and to the generous anonymous readers who helped shape it into what it is today. To my beloved teachers Chandler Alday, Laurie Uttich, R. Mark Hall, and Terry Thaxton: thank you for being the first people to really see me. Thank you to Benjamin Taylor, Richard Locke, and dearest Lis Harris for giving me the tools to tell this story.

Thank you to Seema Reza and the Summer 2023 crew at the Fine Arts Work Center, who gave me the courage to write what would become the opening pages of this book after I'd given up on it so many times. Thank you to the Kenyon Review Young Writers Workshop and the Weekly Faculty Writing Program at Texas Tech for the time and space to write. Thank you to the Humanities Center at Texas Tech for supporting the publication of this book.

Thank you to Alanna Ryder, Jamie Palafox, Melissa Tanis, Nicholas Goodly, Jess Irish, Omar Ortega, Lucy Zhang, Chris Blackman, Michael Juliani, Sam Sodomsky, Kristen Martin, Sheina Elberg, Mushki Grand, Sarah Jackman, Nicole Vigil, Sarah Perry, Wesley Lyons, Danny Maziad, Jen Alex, Jeff Fleisher, Lucy Schiller, Alexandria Caliendo, Roberta Lowe, Amanda Davidson, Heather Bryan, Courtney Ann LaFaive, Melissa Fiegel, Jess Toukatly, Mari Isa, and all the friends and chosen family who have uplifted me in ways big and small over the years. Thank you to

Demian, my fairy godmother, for reminding me that I do come from somewhere. Thank you to Bob, Ron, Angie, Ruben, Roxanna, Abi, Priscilla, Julián, Lucía, and Dodger. To my suegros, Gina and Xavier, gracias por quererme como si fuera su propia hija.

Thank you especially to Amy, Matt, and Amberly Sisneros, our neighbors and friends. You took care of us, clothed us, made us feel safe. Thank you to everyone who visited Nick and me at the hotel that week. If you came over and played cards or board games to distract us. If you dropped off a meal we probably couldn't bear to eat. If you signed a card for us. If you took the time to reach out. Thank you to Reva, my school-appointed psychiatrist from seventh to tenth grade, who took me out of my least favorite class every Tuesday and even came to support me at the trial. I never imagined that writing the acknowledgments of my first book would involve thanking multiple people who are no longer here. I would like to say those names again: Matt and Amy Sisneros, Sarah Jackman, Richard Locke, Reva Heron. I will never forget you.

I wholeheartedly believe I owe my survival to my big brother. Nick, I love you. So much of life with you now feels like resistance. Seeing you laugh, eating McDonald's with you, making a list of how many houses we lived in, remembering a Betty-ism. These things remind me *we survived*. We are capable of joy, of love, in spite of it all. It's what she would want for us. Thank you for saving me and for supporting me in telling this story. I know it's not just mine to tell. I would like to thank my dad, my hero, for teaching me what it means to truly show up. Terry, my champion, for your unwavering support throughout the decades I have known you. You guys gave us a beautiful life when it felt like the whole world had ended.

Thank you to my husband, Nathan Xavier Osorio, my best friend, my first reader and editor (and now photographer!) for everything I do. You made this book possible. You make everything possible. Would it be too much to say you made life worth living?

And finally, Betty: thank you for buying me that copy of *The Outsiders* I still keep in my office now, though I'm sure I will never open it again. Thank you for teaching me that reading and writing are important, that books contain magic. Your brief, brilliant presence in my life often feels like it was just a dream. The existence of this book finally proves it wasn't. Wherever you are, I hope it looks like that painting of all the dogs playing poker. I miss you. I love you.

Previous versions of some sections of the book appear in literary journals, as follows:

"Split Ends" in *Sonora Review*
"Done to Death" in *New Delta Review*
"Doom" in *Blue Mesa Review*
"The Sound of Burning" in *Indiana Review*
"No Contact" in *Hypertext*

CREDITS

Billy Cox, "'What I Encountered That Night Was Pure Evil'; Rolling's Sarasota Rape Victim Survived by Her Wits and Cold Beer," *Sarasota Herald-Tribune*, October 25, 2006. © Billy Cox. Reprinted with permission.

Excerpt from *Shot in the Heart* by Mikal Gilmore, copyright © 1994 by Mikal Gilmore. Used by permission of Doubleday, an imprint of the Knopf Doubleday Publishing Group, a division of Penguin Random House LLC. All rights reserved.

"Gainesville: The Price of Murder," *Turning Point* special episode, 1994, ABC News.

Jason Auslander, "Defendant a 'Time Bomb,'" © 2009, *Santa Fe New Mexican*. All rights reserved. Reprinted with permission.

Lucie Brock-Broido, "A Girl Ago," 2013. Used by permission of Julie Brock Broido and the Estate of Lucie Brock-Broido.

Willow Bay, "Kevin Williamson Enjoying Reign as King of Horror Flicks," NewsStand: CNN & *Entertainment Weekly*, August 7, 1998.

CRUX, THE GEORGIA SERIES IN LITERARY NONFICTION

Debra Monroe, *My Unsentimental Education*
Sonja Livingston, *Ladies Night at the Dreamland*
Jericho Parms, *Lost Wax: Essays*
Priscilla Long, *Fire and Stone: Where Do We Come From? What Are We? Where Are We Going?*
Sarah Gorham, *Alpine Apprentice*
Tracy Daugherty, *Let Us Build Us a City*
Brian Doyle, *Hoop: A Basketball Life in Ninety-Five Essays*
Michael Martone, *Brooding: Arias, Choruses, Lullabies, Follies, Dirges, and a Duet*
Andrew Menard, *Learning from Thoreau*
Dustin Parsons, *Exploded View: Essays on Fatherhood, with Diagrams*
Clinton Crockett Peters, *Pandora's Garden: Kudzu, Cockroaches, and Other Misfits of Ecology*
André Joseph Gallant, *A High Low Tide: The Revival of a Southern Oyster*
Justin Gardiner, *Beneath the Shadow: Legacy and Longing in the Antarctic*
Emily Arnason Casey, *Made Holy: Essays*
Sejal Shah, *This Is One Way to Dance: Essays*
Lee Gutkind, *My Last Eight Thousand Days: An American Male in His Seventies*
Cecile Pineda, *Entry without Inspection: A Writer's Life in El Norte*
Anjali Enjeti, *Southbound: Essays on Identity, Inheritance, and Social Change*
Clinton Crockett Peters, *Mountain Madness: Found and Lost in the Peaks of America and Japan*
Steve Majors, *High Yella: A Modern Family Memoir*
Julia Ridley Smith, *The Sum of Trifles*
Siân Griffiths, *The Sum of Her Parts: Essays*
Ned Stuckey-French, *One by One, the Stars: Essays*
John Griswold, *The Age of Clear Profit: Collected Essays on Home and the Narrow Road*
Debra Monroe, *It Takes a Worried Woman: Essays*
Joseph Geha, *Kitchen Arabic: How My Family Came to America and the Recipes We Brought with Us*
Lawrence Lenhart, *Backvalley Ferrets: A Rewilding of the Colorado Plateau*
Sarah Beth Childers, *Prodigals: A Sister's Memoir of Appalachia*
Jodi Varon, *Your Eyes Will Be My Window: Essays*

Sandra Gail Lambert, *My Withered Legs and Other Essays*
Brooke Champagne, *Nola Face: Memoirs of a Truth-Telling Latina in the Big Easy*
Maddie Norris, *The Wet Wound: An Elegy in Essays*
Cris Mazza, *The Decade of Letting Things Go: A Postmenopause Memoir*
Lydia Paar, *The Exit Is the Entrance: Essays on Escape*
Joe Bonomo, *Play This Book Loud: Noisy Essays*
Wes Jamison, *My Corpse Inside*
Clifford Thompson, *Jazz June: A Self-Portrait in Essays*
Ashley Anderson, *Sifting the Feminine: Essays on a Woman's Body*
Yelizaveta P. Renfro, *The Season of Birds and Stones: Essays*
Alison Kinney, *United States of Rejection: A Story of Love, Hate, and Hope*
Patricia Foster, *A Marriage in Startled Air: A Memoir*
Kristi D. Osorio, *The Sound of Burning: A Mother, a Daughter, a Murder*